COSMOPOLITAN'S

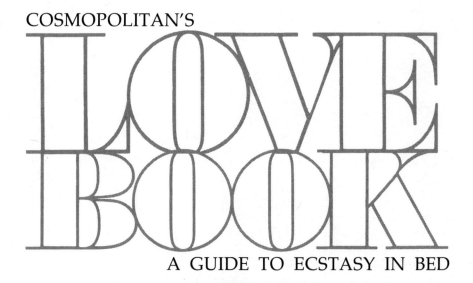

LOVE
BOOK

A GUIDE TO ECSTASY IN BED

COSMOPOLITAN BOOKS • NEW YORK

ACKNOWLEDGMENTS

Many writers contributed to *Cosmopolitan's Love Book,* and we are grateful
to all of them. Specifically we wish to thank the following for permission
to reprint articles that appeared originally in *Cosmopolitan* magazine:
Alma Birk, "Nymphomania"; Jacqueline Brandwynne, "How Sensuous
Should a Working Girl Be?"; Laura Cunningham, "The Power of Touch";
Mopsy Strange Kennedy, "I Was an Overage Virgin"; W. H. Manville,
"Kissing"; Christine Munro, "Getting Deflowered the Second Time
Around," Copyright © 1971 by Irma Kurtz (Christine Munro), reprinted
by permission of The Sterling Lord Agency; Jeannie Sakol, "What Turns
Men On"; Jill Schary, "The Ostentatious Orgasm"; Eugene Schoenfeld,
"Male Insecurities," Copyright © 1971 by Eugene Schoenfeld, reprinted
by permission of The Sterling Lord Agency; Ann Barczay Sloan, "(Sex)
Concentration, Please!"

COSMOPOLITAN BOOKS

Editorial Director *Helen Gurley Brown*

♡ ♡ ♡ ♡ ♡ ♡ ♡ ♡ ♡ ♡ ♡ ♡ ♡ ♡ ♡

Editor-in-Chief *Jeanette Sarkisian Wagner*

Assistant Editor *Veronica Geng*

Copy Editor *Ellen Tabak*

Assistant *Tiena-Kay Halm*

Contents

FOREWORD

*H*ere, we hope, is the ultimate *love* book . . . not a sex text—although it *will* revolutionize your sex life if you really do all we tell you! Sexuality is *not* a mechanical thing. If an orgasm were your only goal, an electric vibrator could help you achieve that, *technically*. But what any woman *really* wants is so much more . . . more human, more beautiful, more fulfilling, more magical, more mystical, more supportive. She craves the intimate sharing between two people. And it's love that turns two people into one. We believe in this joining, sharing, commitment, as we *don't* believe in group sex where the personal *meaning* of love is corrupted.

*T*hus, this book is a guide to loving. In it you'll find expert advice on how you can understand and love your own body, how to entice men to adore you passionately, ways to sustain lust, how the erotic senses work, every beautiful thing that two loving people can do in bed, how to turn anyone into a better lover, and more!

*F*ollow us, step by step, through a growing process that will help you achieve your fullest potential as a pleasure-feeling, pleasure-giving woman, *not* a sex-object. After all, male-female sex needn't be sexist! We all desire and need one another . . . and both sexes are entitled to be splendidly ecstatic in bed. So hug this book to your pretty bosom and let it help you become your most beautiful, sensuous, lovable-and-loving self.

Helen Gurley Brown

Editor-in-Chief
COSMOPOLITAN

Awakening
your
sensuality

ONE

What does it take to be sensuous? Must you experience a hundred lovers, a thousand multi-orgasms? Is it essential for your measurements to be 36-24-36? Should you grow a wild mane of Raquel Welch hair, unbutton your blouse below your cleavage?

No. No. No. A sensuous woman is more than a sexy woman. She might still be a virgin, or have had the average girl's experience—a few affairs, some splendid, some gruesome, some merely boring. Yes, she could be a honey-haired, shapely goddess, but she's more likely to be a little too thin, or a trifle too fat, with a mole on her nose or a wig on her head. Fortunately, there are few goddesses and *more* of us pleasantly imperfect types walking around. Sensuality does not depend on beauty, age, or wealth.

Sensuality starts, for women as well as men, in the sexual organs, the genitals. If you've cringed at those words—if you've ever blushed or re-coiled at the words *vagina, clitoris, vulva, penis, scrotum*—you're not sen-suous. For sensuality indeed does begin in those places, moving outward and, yes, in the best cases, finally encompassing body *and* soul. The special awareness of sensuality's origins adds a tenderness to your touch, your speech . . . the way you move . . . a tenderness that men respond to. They sense sexuality at a glance, and it warms them. A sensuous woman feels a deep yearning to love the right man, expresses an openness, a *willing-*ness to explore all the *possible* candidates.

Men always think a sensuous girl is pretty, even if her face and figure are ordinary. They don't really "see" her; instead they respond to the sub-liminal signals her entire body sends. Nonsensuous women frequently are astonished to hear men admire these girls. "You can't mean that little-nothing Jane?" Ah, but he does, because there's something about Jane that makes him want to hold her and make love to her.

A sensuous woman will be blessed with love throughout her life and will grow lovelier with age, because sensuality *ripens* . . . slowly, deliciously . . . flowing from its warm source, enhancing everything.

Now let's see how sensuous *you* are:
- Have you ever held a man's head in your lap while he slept?
- Do you ache inside when certain special men look at you?
- Are you able to insert a diaphragm or tampon without using an applicator?
- Do you like to be admired in the nude?
- Can you make love with the lights on?
- Do you think a naked man can be beautiful?
- Do you enjoy having someone brush your hair?
- Will you sleep with a man as soon as you *feel* like it? Even if it's the first date?
- Do you have a few dear, *female* friends?
- Have you enjoyed touching your own genitals?
- Can you have sexual relations without "faking" climax?
- Do you like touching people other than your lover?
- Do you find kittens and puppies irresistible?

You should answer an emphatic "Yes!" to all these questions. If you're sensuous, you find nothing repulsive about your own vagina and clitoris, love your body, and like men. Around the right man, you overflow with warmth and tenderness. Just looking at a very special man can send an orgasmic shiver up your spine. You don't demand gifts, dates, and phony promises in exchange for your body. You value yourself and consider your body a gift given generously in exchange only for your pleasure. Lastly, you love sex, love feeling a man's strong body next to yours, the thrust of a man inside you . . . and you enjoy moving rhythmically against him. The passive ragdoll isn't *your* style; you initiate sex about half the time, consider your desire and needs as urgently important as a man's! Aware that seduction is one of the most *delicious* aspects of lovemaking, you vamp your man whenever you want him. It's sensuous to be liberated. Junk that outmoded idea that man dominates woman in bed. Stop thinking of sex as something he *does* to you. Sex is to be enjoyed together—both giving, both taking . . . craving, arching, tightening, and finally exploding . . . ultimate pleasure. It's more than orgasm—sex is the unique feeling you have for your man, the special tensions that spark from his body to yours.

page 4

Being sexy/sensuous doesn't interfere with being smart. Dumb blondes are outdated. Today's sexpot is *brainy* and *accomplished,* very much the equal of any similarly endowed man. Probably the *more* intelligent she is, the *more* sensuous it's possible to be . . . because she can *learn* how to develop her innate womanliness.

Don't feel depressed if your sensuality isn't sufficiently ripened. Cultural prejudices and personal inhibitions can do much to keep a healthy libido down, all potential locked inside. Blocks—psychological and social—keep many men and women out of touch with their own flesh and the ways to enjoy lovemaking. If you haven't had sex, or have experienced only bad or indifferent sex, we'll suggest specifics to help you. This book is for you as much as it is for the girl who's had many happy affairs.

Read on to find out how to create and enjoy the sexiest life you've ever known . . . how to shed nasty inhibitions, explore your eroticism, develop your naked body, excite yourself to passion, thrill a man, and become a better lover yourself.

Sexual muddles
and
fallacies

TWO

Until now, sex books have concentrated on rather exotic problems, dwelling on morbid psychological traumas or bizarre physical conditions. Case histories abound of girls whose vaginas snap shut before penetration and who need psychological help to let their muscles unclench. That particularly uptight situation is called *vaginismus*. Yes, there *is* such a problem. But it is very, very rare. Alas, sex books overemphasize some obscure problems and overlook simple every-night dilemmas: How to relax and feel confident enough to have an orgasm? Who to sleep with? How to gain sexual finesse . . . without losing that spark of spontaneous lust? And so on. These problems need to be faced regularly.

I'm not suggesting that special sexual problems be ignored; any girl who has a severe physical or psychological problem should recognize it and get proper medical help immediately. This book is not for her. It is a basic guide to typical, every-night sexual problems and how to fix them. Cos-MOPOLITAN's staff polled hundreds of girls whose experience is probably like yours. They're not Hottentot natives, harem mates, or former call girls, but young, hip career women who want a good sex life. And these young women, it was found, often worry over the *same things*. Mainly, they are still a bit self-conscious in bed, and may have a few inhibitions regarding their bodies or a male's body. Most girls still cling to a few common sexual fallacies. Do you think these statements are true or false?

- A virgin always has a hymen.
- You lose interest in sex when you get older.
- There is a difference between clitoral and vaginal orgasm.
- It's unhealthy to have sex during your period.
- You should douche after sex.
- If a man withdraws before orgasm, you can't get pregnant.

- Only prostitutes and degenerates get venereal disease.
- Only animals have sex with the male approaching from the rear.
- Oral sex is unhygienic.
- You can have sex too often.

All of these are sexual misconceptions, yet this very minute there are probably many girls saying "no" to their lovers because they're menstruating . . . and other girls saying "yes" to lovers who promise to "pull out in time." Thousands of girls are scurrying into bathrooms clutching their douche bags when they could be in bed cuddling close to their lovers. And who knows how many women are brooding over the "*right* kind of orgasm." Is there a *wrong* kind? No! Unnecessary *angst*.

To banish these silly, destructive sexual fallacies, get the facts. Here are some crucial ones:

• *The hygiene mystique: Intercourse is dirty, you must wash immediately afterward. You are unclean while menstruating. Oral sex spreads germs.*
Fact: Sex is a *natural* function, and no special *cleanup* is required. Douching is used to help clean vaginal infections (more on this later). You don't need to douche after sex.

Your menstrual flow, far from being dirty, is actually *antiseptic*. Whether you and your lover want to make love during your period is a question of personal preference. Since the female sex urge skyrockets during this time, it's likely you will. The only real problem here is the bed linen—not you. You may want to put a towel over the sheet to protect it, or wear a diaphragm to hold back the flow. Many people have coitus during this time and should stop feeling guilty about it. However, contraception *should* be used, for in many instances the period isn't as "safe" as has long been assumed. Now, as for oral sex, it's no less hygienic than genital sex. In fact, the extra lubrication from oral-genital kisses helps prevent chafing during sexual intercourse.

• *There are wrong ways of lovemaking. Some positions are animalistic. Too much sex is unhealthy.*
Fact: The only *right* position is the one that makes both lovers happy. About-face if you wish. So-called "animal-like" positions are *human!* You *can't* have too much sex. Your body will crave only as much sex as it can handle . . . then you'll fall asleep. Clinically, a woman *could* exhaust fifty men a night, but *usually* one man is enough.

Every aspect of sexuality has its own long list of misconceptions, myths, and fallacies. Consider some of these:

• *Liquor is a marvelous sexual stimulant.* Alas, liquor is a depressant, not a stimulant, and taken in any large quantities, sexually incapacitates any lover. Many a honeymoon's first night has been ruined because the fearful husband has drunk himself into a stupor to quell his anxieties and been unable to have an erection even though his sex urge was powerful! And although a woman asleep, drunk, or even dead is capable of sexual intercourse as a passive receiver, the chances of reaching any orgasm are small. Alcohol deadens all nerve centers . . . including the sexual ones!

A drink or *two,* however, may help an anxious man or woman release certain sexual inhibitions, or at least lessen tension caused by other events of the day. (And, of course, cocktails are festive and romantic.) But if you find you *always* need liquor to surmount sexual inhibitions, it would be far smarter to seek psychotherapeutic help.

• A battery of myths exists about breasts and sex: All of the following statements are *false! Sexual response in women is directly related to breast size. Women with tiny breasts can't have orgasms. Women with huge mammaries can't have orgasms. Women with huge breasts are sexier.* What silliness! The United States is a breast culture, and all it symbolically represents (Mommy, of course!) is idealized and fantasized. The breasts are not highly erogenous zones, but the nipples *are.* Regardless of variations in breast size, the nipples on all women are usually the *same* size, and nipple size doesn't determine how excited you can get or how many orgasms you can have. The only importance about breast size in sex is what each *man* prefers. That's his problem, not yours. And if you know a man like the one in the film *Carnal Knowledge* who equates sex with an E-cup brassiere, forget him. He's sexually immature and will end, as does the "hero" of that film, nearly impotent! Who needs that?!

• *Having orgasms in your dreams means you're sexually disturbed.* Nonsense! Both men and women have them . . . as a perfectly healthy release from sexual tensions.

• *It's possible to learn a master love technique that will work for every man and woman.* Impossible! No two of us is alike, much less craving exactly the same thing every time we make love. Love is spontaneous, the delicious discovery of what special things you do that excite your lover. Routine lovemaking becomes only boring eventually, even if it produced orgasms at the onset. With sex experiences, our tastes and needs vary. Explore possibilities . . . and enjoy them.

• *Menstruating women shouldn't bathe, shower, play active sports, or engage in intercourse.* What a silly waste of time, and a demonstration of ignorance. It is far healthier to work and play as usual. Menstruation isn't an illness, but a natural body function that in no way impairs your ability to do anything. Incredible myths surround the menstrual process and are believed by many young men and women, including such nonsense as: *If an impotent man performs cunnilingus on a menstruating woman, his potency will return.* Bah!

• *When two people are in love, they'll automatically be good lovers.* Not necessarily so. Liking good food doesn't make you a gourmet cook! Some people are terrific sex technicians who know little of love, only the mechanics of the sexual act itself. And others who adore each other and want to please in every way simply don't know where to start or what to do. That's one of the reasons for this book . . . to help you be a good lover when you love someone. You need to learn certain fundamental sexual techniques to help you express love sexually to a man . . . but remember sexual skill is only one way of expressing love or being a good lover. A cheerfulness of spirit, a desire to really relate to a man in every part of his life and interests, not merely the physical, to spare him pain and give him joy . . . by word, by touch, by gesture, by action . . . all of those are aspects of love. Sex as an expression of love is so much more meaningful than the mere act of union.

But remember that even if you love each other deeply, you won't be in perfect harmony constantly. Sometimes one partner's need for sex is strongly physical, not merely an extension of an exalted state of loving. Don't expect skyrockets every time. Sex often is needed to ease anxiety, insecurity, to feel reassured and competent.

The list of really crazy sex muddles is endless . . . but here are some of those reported most often by doctors (notably in Dr. James Leslie McCary's excellent book *Sexual Myths and Fallacies* (Van Nostrand Reinhold). All the following are false!

• *Blonde women have greater sexual potential.*
• *Your nose determines your vaginal size and consequent interest in sex.*
• *It's only proper for a man to initiate lovemaking, never a woman.* Nonsense! Don't you love being wanted, needed, desired? Doesn't it make you feel special, sexy, happy? Why shouldn't you help a man to feel the same way?

Of course you should . . . not only for his sake, but yours as well. You are not the second sex any more; your urges and needs are as normal as his, and you have a right to express them, to want sex, to have it, and to be fulfilled by it. One marvelous, heady way to arouse yourself is to start making love to a man, gently, delicately, stroking every part of his body lightly as a feather, lingering in no single place, surprising him with your sporadic kisses . . . on his eyelids, inner thigh, the arch of his foot, small of his back, nape of his neck, and every other part of him that appeals to you. As you watch his arousal, you'll feel enormously powerful and sexy yourself! At other times, you'll want *him* to reciprocate. Fine.

• *Handsome, athletic men are really the best lovers.* Not necessarily. There is no correlation between muscles and lovemaking ability. In fact, many athletic men have diverted much of their sexual interest to sports and are not so competent as their flabby brothers. Those particularly addicted to body-building are too narcissistic to make good lovers. Many of them harbor profound feelings of inadequacy that make for complicated sex problems.

• *Men with large amounts of body hair are very, very sexy.*
• *The best health is enjoyed by those who abstain from sex.*
• *Orgasm is necessary for conception.*
• *If a man or woman is sterilized, sex drive diminishes.*
• *Older men and women should not expect to enjoy sexual experiences.*
• *Having a hysterectomy ends a woman's ability to enjoy sex.*
• *Unusual or excessive sexual practices can lead to mental breakdown.*
• *Pornography corrupts the minds and actions of everyone—and especially of little children.*

All the above statements are myths, totally false. Banish them from your mind forever!

Sometimes a sexual fallacy is even more than a mistaken idea. Whole attitudes can be unrealistic or unfounded. Such muddles may make you unhappy in bed. It's a wonder, with all the books, talk, and pseudo-sexual diversions these days, that anyone has the leftover time or interest actually to go to bed and explore the delights of another person's body. I doubt that any couple gets together without a lot of authoritative notions cluttering up their own free responses.

Probably one of the major muddles concerns orgasms. The orgasm is defined in one dictionary as: " . . . immoderate or eager excitement or action, especially the culmination of coition." A rather delicate and coy definition, that—the word "immoderate" thrown in, I think, to satisfy our Calvinist ethics. Orgasm has also been described as a release of sexual and nervous tension, related most closely to the sneeze.

The adjective "ostentatious" is used to describe the first type of orgasm we'll be discussing, but it can also apply to the preeminent role the orgasm plays in contemporary male-female relationships.

A few years ago, *Esquire* magazine published an article about the big O, criticizing emphasis on orgasmic achievement as a status symbol and a *cause célèbre*. It's pretty difficult to dismiss the subject in a flip manner, however, if one considers the number of marriages (and other relationships) that fall apart because of sexual incompatibility.

It may well be true that overemphasis creates tensions and conflicts that might have remained below the surface or been sublimated in another era. But our generation is, if anything, the Open Generation, and we can no longer tolerate the myths and clotted proprieties of former ages.

The orgasm may seem ostentatious only because for the first time in history it can be discussed openly. The ability and right of women as well as men to enjoy sexual expression and satisfaction is as important and relevant a subject today as any other physical ability or civil right.

However, mention the word "orgasm" in some circles and eyebrows still go up two inches, women giggle or look guilty, and men look vaguely hostile or protective. From the defensive silence that ensues, you get the feeling, with married couples particularly, that the subject is simply not discussed, at least not with each other. It's about time these defenses came down: What we have here, as you've heard a lot, is a failure to communicate. No excuse!

William H. Masters, M.D., and Mrs. Virginia E. Johnson, in their remarkable book *Human Sexual Response* (published by Little, Brown and Company in 1966), which you should read, proved that there are clearly visible physiological changes that occur as a woman approaches and achieves orgasm. However, it is entirely unlikely that any couple has the scientific detachment necessary to check on all these phases. It would somehow detract from the fun if a man suddenly whipped out a stethoscope or started winding one of those blood-pressure things around the woman's arm, or darted at her with a flashlight (unless, of course, they dig playing doctor). I think, therefore, it is safe to say that many women do pretend, with various amounts of conscious efforts—at least sometimes. Pretense does not necessarily mean that a woman is totally, calculatedly feigning every sigh or reaction; she may be quite involved or stimulated but simply not getting all the way there. She may be having a perfectly delightful time and be, to a certain measure, quite satisfied.

The Ostentatious Orgasm is probably more prevalent in relationships outside marriage. As a man wants to prove his masculinity, so a woman, in this way, may need to prove her femininity. She may bring to bed many inhibitions, tensions, and insecurities that prohibit the total involvement needed for orgasm. During the first few times with any given man, she may find it easier to fake, hoping that as the relationship deepens, her response will grow, or she will be able, when she knows him better and trusts him more, to communicate her particular sexual wishes and needs without reserve.

Sexual dialogue can be very revealing:
HE (apprehensively): Did you . . . ?
SHE (sighing): Oh, at least a hundred times . . . I mean it.

A perceptive man will think, "Oh, sure." He will recognize her self-consciousness and try to break through the barriers that cause this affectation without, it's to be hoped, any miserable confrontation like, "Why are you lying?" She would probably say, "I'm not," and even more barriers would be built up. We are all probably more vulnerable about our sexuality than anything else—terrified of being teased or rebuked. This, more than any other fact, is equally true of both sexes. It's hard to be too sensitive or overconsiderate of another's feelings.

The major problem with the Ostentatious Orgasm, apart from the obvious —that physical tensions are not being released—is that it creates a wall between the man and the woman. As time goes on, it is increasingly difficult for her to admit something is wrong. Depending upon her basic personality, she may feel she is cheating him or she may develop a smug attitude like "I fooled him again," which can turn into out-and-out contempt. A dreary, hopeless resignation may set in, and eventually it will be too much effort to pretend at all.

She may resolve at some point in the relationship, "Next time I'll really try, and I *won't* fake it." But she may be pretty well locked into a performance, a habit really, and find it impossible to break away, afraid he will think she has cooled; she doesn't want to ruin any relationship they may have built on her performance.

Solution: Probably the best way out of the Ostentatious Orgasm bag is to suggest gently, with some seductive urgency, that there has been something else you'd like to try: Say that you've had a fantasy about such and such, whatever it is that you think would work. If he's worth your being there in the first place, he'll very likely go along. He may not know what or why, but he'll probably sense a difference in your response, and without employing any scientific method, either.

Orgasmic pleasure is not measured in decibels or square yards of thrashing around. A deep, satisfying orgasm can be a still, silent experience. Most men know this, if not instinctively, at least from experience. Of course, there's always the exception. One girl told me that her lover would be very disappointed if she didn't shout and scream. So after her orgasm subsided, she would shout and scream for a few moments; then he could relax, quite pleased with himself. She said, however, that he was exceptionally proud when her shouts would bring neighbors pounding on the door. So maybe he was a bit of an exhibitionist, who knows? As long as none of the neighbors died of fright, I suppose that's one form of Ostentatious Orgasm that worked out well for both parties (if not for anyone upstairs trying to get some sleep; but then, everyone loves a lover, yes?)

Another kind of orgasm is the one you want your *friends* to think you are having. Never mind how it really was, what you're really all excited about is inducing a little jealousy in your friends by making them think you're the most responsive thing this side of flypaper.

No matter which sex goes in for it, this sort of bedtime story is transparent and depressing. People who are having a really incredible time in bed usually have reached a point of such frank and open intimacy in every sense (no pun intended) that they have neither the need nor the desire to tell *anyone* about it. Any discussion would be an invasion of their very special closeness. Genuine sexuality does not need a press agent. It seems one thing to discuss sex with a very close friend (ideally, your lover), another to discuss the general aspects of sex and orgasm and what it all means with just a friend-friend (O.K. once in a while), and yet something *else* to proclaim one's own prowess to *anybody*.

For many women the discussion of sex in itself is probably a turn-on, verbal foreplay. Constant talk about sex by one girl to another may be an unconscious game. Her orgasms may, indeed, be only ostentatious, but her motives for discussion of same, however subtle, are rather insidious. Her integrity to her lover seems rather less important than her desire to sell her girl friend(s) on her seductive abilities.

In all relationships between people of the same or opposite sex, we tend to be closest to those we consider in some way attractive. There is always an awareness of a friend's sexual appeal, whether we admit it or not. There's a degree of *latent* homosexuality in all human beings; accepting and understanding this for what it is, without fear, is healthy.

A girl fixing her friend's hair feels a warmth and closeness that is partly sexual. But she'd be mortified, probably, if her friend made any obvious sexual advances. Instead, they release their feelings about each other—again, probably unconsciously—by talking about their heterosexual love lives. In these conversations they place an emphasis upon their own responses, not the man's, almost as if the girl is to be jealous of *him,* rather than jealous of her friend.

There was a wistful man I knew once who said the trouble with sex is that only a woman can really understand another woman's body. (That's a rationalization some lesbians use to justify their behavior—if they feel they must.) Actually, a woman who understands her own body can help any man understand it; and when he does, he understands it very well indeed if she lets him. The point here is that girls who persist in the Ostentatious Orgasm syndrome (varieties A and B, which are often related) usually don't try to be understood because they may not really like men very much. Men can be brainwashed by some women, not loved or given a chance. Such girls use their sexual energies in self-promotion, not genuine involvement.

Many girls have been led to believe that the "clitoral" orgasm is, somehow, infantile, immature, and insignificant. The words "I'm sorry, but it's the only way I can . . . " echo this mournful thought. Some evidently narrow-minded, underexperienced psychologists and authors of marriage manuals deserve a complimentary head-to-toe outfit of tar and feathers for having created this particular myth many years ago. A quick refresher course in female anatomy is indicated: The clitoris is the female equivalent of the male organ, constructed in a similar fashion, including the same complement of highly concentrated nerve endings, which the inner wall of the vagina does not have, possibly because it could not function as effectively as a birth canal if it did.

I'm not trying to put together a sexual reference library for you—I'd really rather have you find out these things for yourself—but if you haven't been learning anything firsthand, try to find a copy of *Sex: Methods and Manners,* by Louis Berg and Robert Street (Macfadden). It says, for instance:

page 17

> . . . by far the most important region of the entire female
> body for inducing passion and effecting sexual gratification
> is the clitoris . . . No man can be a qualified lover who is not
> thoroughly familiar with the power and peculiarities of this
> tiny and powerful organ.

The vast influence of the anticlitoris cult was shown by Dr. Alfred C. Kinsey when he said, "There are hundreds of women disturbed because they are unable to accomplish the anatomical impossibility of 'transferring' their clitoral reactions to vaginal response." Masters and Johnson in *Human Sexual Response* discredit the myth by stating there is no biological difference in response between "clitoral" and "vaginal" orgasm. Simply stated, an orgasm is an orgasm. Freudian psychologists falsely believed that orgasm reached by masturbation of the clitoris was an "immature" orgasm. The truth is that the highest-intensity orgasm is produced through masturbation of the clitoral area. Upon stimulation of the clitoris by any means, the vagina reacts orgasmically whether a penis is inside it or not (though many women receive extra *psychological* pleasure when a man's penis is inside them).

There is no doubt that a well-trained and practiced vaginal musculature is an important factor in sexual pleasure for both man and woman. One basic exercise is very simple and involves the muscles that control the bladder. Take a deep breath, draw in and up the lower region of your body, keep drawing up. Let go, start again, and you've got it. If done consistently and properly, this exercise will produce a dizzy, tingling feeling, and—in the right place, at the right time—a definite orgasmic satisfaction. The release may not be so specifically dynamic as that achieved by clitoral stimulation, but the muscle-flexing greatly enchances male pleasure; and despite female pleasure and satisfaction being newly emphasized these days with much talk about male obligation, a great deal of your own delight will come from knowing you are giving him a special kind of love. (See Chapter Five for more on self-stimulation.)

What about obligatory orgasm? The dialogue goes something like this:
HE: Well, did you?
SHE: Oh, it's all right.
HE: No, it isn't really fair this way.
SHE: No . . . really, you're tired.

The *silent* thoughts go like this:
HE: She'll be cross as hell all day.
SHE: I guess I should have pretended.

He: If I don't, she'll feel rejected.
She: If I don't let him, he'll feel rejected.

And so, what is supposed to be a pleasant release of tensions becomes a tension-producing game. Both are trying so hard that neither gets anywhere. And even if the game finally works, so much attention has been paid to the *object* of the exercise that it became just that: exercise. Sex, above all, should be fun. If it winds up as work, it loses spontaneity, and this can make any relationship deteriorate. Sex should not be a matter of chalking up equal-orgasm time.

The ultimate example here is that of the couple who built up so much anxiety and tension over *her* orgasm that they went to bed with a timer set at five minutes. If she couldn't make it by the time allotted, they called the game and retired to their own sides. The wife in this case said all she could think of were the minutes ticking off, and all he could think of, she imagined, was how much longer it would take, and the only thing turned on was the timer.

Sex, of course, can be a tonic, and is one of the healthiest escapes around. There's a danger in touting its beneficial qualities, of course, because sex is more fun when you think it's just plain fun. So even if you know, and he knows you know, that it's a therapy session because you're tense, nervous, on edge—keep quiet and let the passion take over. Don't talk so much. Have a couple of drinks or listen to some music, then go to bed. Making sex work is like talking about making marriage work: It puts the emphasis on a laborious concentration that will only destroy what should be total and unrestrained giving.

On the other hand, if your partner is in the mood, go along, not as conscious therapy, but more because you dig the person and would like to make him or her feel marvelous. You think each other's bodies are intriguing delights. Making those delights into therapy only distorts the emphasis. No one should have to be told to make love . . . but there's nothing wrong with asking sweetly.

There is another orgasm game:
She: You go ahead, I don't feel like it, but I want to please you, I enjoy
        just being with you. . . .
He: But half the pleasure is giving you pleasure, too.

This situation may result in an Ostentatious Orgasm if she feigns pleasure and doesn't say anything.

"But you know how I am," she says, having thereby convinced herself she won't achieve it.

"Never say die," says he, having convinced himself she's going to.

Now sex becomes a contest, which may actually be a fantasy of hers that both recognize without consciously understanding what it's all about. Perhaps she fantasizes she's a virgin, possibly because she feels sex is more fun when it's bad, possibly because she always heard it was; and he is the expert lover who is going to release her from her prison tower, or the curious paradox, the gentle rapist who insists on turning her on first because it makes him feel better. This way she takes no responsibility for any guilts she may unconsciously have about sex. It's a fine game if both have a sort of silent agreement, but it can hit a blind alley if *he* wants to be seduced. In a really good sexual relationship, fantasies take turns, and each partner can assume either side of a given fantasy.

But what a bore if she just lies there blankly with a "Take me—show me" expression, expecting, demanding, that he alone always carry them along with inventive dialogue and enough sex drive for both. Obviously, that's going to unnerve any man if it continues. She might better introduce elements of the Ostentatious Orgasm and get involved; before she knows it, she will be.

Another pet project of marriage-manual authors is the foolish notion it is absolutely vital to the success of any marriage (they don't recognize relationships) for the couple to have simultaneous orgasm. I have visions of couples with little gold whistles, saying, "Now, ready, get set, and GO!" If everyone is busy concentrating on this goal, they probably won't reach it at *all*.

And if you're having a wonderful time, does it really matter? If it does matter to you so terribly much, you're on the merry-go-round for the brass ring and not for the ride and the music and all that. In our society we are conditioned, of course, to want only the best, and they call this, somewhere, the Quality Orgasm. But orgasm is neither quality nor quantity; it's a happening, maybe, and you are both artists who enjoy putting the happening on as much as you do seeing it all finished. Maybe even more.

People have enough trouble concentrating on sex without worrying about precision formation. I don't know why this is, but making love is not necessarily a well-coordinated activity. At best it is too spontaneous, too free. At worst it is pleasurable but awkward. If a woman thinks it is all *that* important to a man that they experience at least one mutual, simultaneous orgasm, she might as well enlist the aid of an easily regulated Ostentatious Orgasm. Otherwise, any effort spent on this alleged treasure is most likely to wind up in frustration and, perhaps, remorseful apologies, silent accusations, and so forth. If it is going to happen, it will, accidentally, when both of you least expect it.

Men used to be told they'd grow hair on their palms, or worse, if they masturbated. Girls weren't told anything, because a girl wouldn't even dream of such a thing. That's because, in those days, women weren't supposed to have orgasms, and everyone played the game by pretending they didn't. Actually, at one point in history, women suspected of having orgasms were likely to be arrested for witchcraft.

Well, girls do masturbate; it's one of the ways they learn about their own bodies so that when the time comes they can then explain it all to their men. Masters and Johnson, in fact, claim that women who masturbate are able to achieve orgasm more rapidly. The lesson here is likely that such a woman is more relaxed and less inhibited—she may indulge in her own fantasies more freely. Ideally, a woman gets to a point with a man where she is just as comfortable with him as she is with herself.

Another favorite myth of the marriage manuals is that female masturbation decreases her chances of later sexual happiness (which, of course, she is *only* to have after marriage, for heaven's sake!) because she learns to rely on her own techniques. More likely, without masturbation she'll fear she might be frigid, or experience a naïveté about the feel and perfume of her own body, or a total unawareness of any aspect of sexuality.

Excuse the repetition, but self-consciousness and inhibitions have *no* place in the bedroom or wherever you are. Remember, he's as fascinated with your body as you are. (Does that have to be such a secret?) Just admit you are, and you'll be on the right track.

We all indulge in fantasies. One of the best examples of what men and women are really up to in bed is a tableau (oh, that's a three-dimensional life-size sculpture, sort of) by Edward Kienholz called "Visions of Sugar Plums." It depicts a bedroom, furnished in bad thirties "blonde moderne," complete with peach chenille spread and round-mirrored vanity. In the bed are two mannequins, making love in the so-called conventional manner. Their heads are huge flesh-colored papier-mâché balloons. You can look through a hole in the top of each one and see a miniature tableau. Inside his head is a Ken doll (the quasi-male Barbie) being crawled all over by a highly unruly group of Barbie dolls. Inside her head is a Barbie doll, standing naked and quite prim before a long line of Ken dolls, who are all at attention waiting their turn. Many people feel this "vision" is really sad, illustrating the lack of communication between men and women. I think, on the other hand, it shows a healthy honesty about the fact that people making love are two individuals bringing their fantasies together in separate, equal pleasure.

In fantasizing, it is possible to get overinvolved. The case in point: an actress who said by the time she had everything staged just right— costumes, sets, and large cast—the whole thing was over. That's an Over-dressed Orgasm.

Sometimes, too, the acting out of a fantasy can completely vitiate its effect: What was imagined turns out to be not nearly so sexy in real life. But some attempt at understanding each other's fantasies should be made. To people who care about each other, nothing should seem obscene, ridiculous, or alarming. Any confidence, given and taken in sincerity and trust, will only serve to make you closer . . . and foolish talk brings depression and anguish:

HE: That was good. . . .
SHE: Do you really love me, or is it just sex?
HE: Yes.
SHE: Yes, what?
HE: Yes, I guess I love you.
SHE: Don't you know?
HE: Of course . . .
SHE: What does it mean to you?
HE: What does what mean?
SHE: Our being together like this.
HE: Having sex?
SHE: How can you say it, so, well, crudely? It is more than that, isn't it?
HE: I just said so.
SHE: Oh. Well, if we couldn't make love, would you still want to be with me?
HE: I can't just separate it like that.
SHE: Well, then it is just sex.
HE: Hey, let's get some sleep.
SHE: I mean nothing to you.

Do be quiet. Put your arms around him and go to sleep. Men—and any generalization is dangerous, but this is about one of the safest—are less talkative than women, especially about their feelings, their emotions concerning their women, or even the one woman. They've been culturally conditioned to be that way. You may be able to help him be more expressive over the long run, but meanwhile, *accept* him. If you're deeply insecure about his feelings, you shouldn't be there. And by the same logic, if you're with him because he's attractive and it's fun and that's that, resist the temptation to make a federal case out of it. You're there because touching and being touched is lovely. If both of you feel more than that, you'll *know,* and shouldn't need constant reassurance.

If meaningfulness must come up (before, during, or after making love), you're dwelling on the future, the past, tomorrow morning, and a dozen other things. Fine if you *both* agree to do so . . . otherwise, one of you is dissatisfied with the whole *premise* of your relationship, and hadn't you better clear up that basic misunderstanding?

If you're hung up on the insecure-romantic role, orgasm won't be what you think it ought to be. You may have been reading too many novels, and you're expecting no less than a personal apocalypse, complete with raging waves of flame, shooting stars, surging tides of golden lava, or however it was described in the latest best seller. You're thinking (too much) that maybe if he *really* loved you, sex would be more like *that,* whatever "that" currently is.

Everyone, of course, would describe an orgasm differently. Music, rather than words, describes it best, and you've heard orgasmic expression a dozen or more times in every kind of music from jazz to rock to symphony. If you've had an orgasm, and you'll know if you have, you'll understand. But if perhaps you don't know, orgasm begins with a gentle humming sensation, a gathering, growing feeling that flows up and through your body, suddenly explodes and melts all over—an intense, warm flush—then subsides with a rocking beat.

There is no such thing as a more or less spiritual orgasm, no matter how sublime your relationship. The *physical* response may be just as intense with someone you aren't *that* involved with. (Your *psychological* response, of course, may be profoundly different.) Orgasm may be stronger or weaker, depending on the amount of physical and psychic stimulation. It will vary with your mood, your health, and so forth. Your interest in him will, of course, augment your feelings, before and after; that's an important part of what sex is all about. But please, don't *demand* poetic words, inspirational tributes, or choral overtures with every orgasm. And don't compete under the covers.

Sex is not the Kentucky Derby or a pie-eating contest. There's a song from *Annie Get Your Gun* called "Anything You Can Do, I Can Do Better." While women usually have more complicated orgasms and *may* take more time getting started, they are often able not only to have multiple orgasms but also to make love all night (or day, or both).

Few men over the age of, say, thirty, are able to continue, technically, making love, more than once or twice. Circumstances and individuals may prove the exception. *Understand* this, without making sympathetic noises, feeling inadequate or unwanted, or teasing him in any way. If you feel unsatisfied, relax, hold him in your arms, and wait for your tension to subside. It will.

A well-known psychiatrist stated about a year ago that during the thirties, forties, and early fifties, the majority of his patients were women complaining of frigidity (which was generally not frigidity, but a lack of understanding between husband and wife). However, he said, during recent years his patients have been mostly men complaining about impotence, usually due to male fear that the woman was "overaggressive."

There's a fine line between letting him know you are interested and browbeating. And there are many ways to accomplish either. Letting him know how interested you are is done by gestures, gentle affection, and all the other things you already know about seduction. Browbeating is done with comparisons about how often so-and-so makes love, or how long it's been since, or cynical remarks about maybe getting another lover—"if you're going to be like this."

Actually, there is no such thing as too much sex, for either of you, provided both are reasonably interested. If you are making love and it is apparent that he is not aroused, *don't* tease. As you loathe being made fun of, never make fun of a man. Share ideas and be willing to experiment, but don't pressure him if he's not in the mood for a particular form of expression. Don't put him down if he suggests something you were conditioned to believe was wrong or bad or dirty. No activity between two people who find each other exciting or wonderful is any of those things, despite some archaic laws we still have in some of our "enlightened" states. A little civil disobedience between friends can be lovely.

Being open, free, and frank with each other is obviously most important, but none of these objectives precludes gentleness—a highly desirable quality that has every bit as much to do with sex as the ability to have an orgasm. The orgasm lasts only a brief time; while a mutually sensitive relationship can satisfy for years. Don't give those years up for the seconds of pleasure you can have next week. Just concentrate on communicating with a little more honesty, a lot more gentleness.

All these sexual muddles and fallacies are the output of a desexed society. Only recently has sexual liberation raged over our country like a forest fire. The flare-up of interest in nudity, sexuality on stage, X-rated movies, blatantly crude underground newspapers, is all the more intense because it follows a sixty-year drought. Overt sex was repressed during the Victorian era. Your grandmothers probably went to their wedding nights as virgin brides in enormous ignorance about a man's body as well as the sexual act. Your mother probably fared better if she tossed her fringy skirts as a flapper and joined the "Everybody's doin' it, doin' it" gang. But more likely, she sedately married your father without ever having much sex experience beyond *necking*.

*W*ell, now it's your turn. In theory, you should have more and better sexual information than your female antecedents, thus more fulfilling sexual experiences. But in practice, you may still have some vestigial inhibitions from previous up-tight generations.

I assume your upbringing was modern. No one told you you'd get warts if you masturbated. But still, no one provided clear information about your sexual desires. There probably were no strict lectures on "decency" and "keeping pure," but your parents didn't invite boys to "sleep over" either. And while some young things today are being outfitted with the Pill at age thirteen, you were not so well equipped. Fear of pregnancy cramped your style, along with all the unspoken warnings against premarital sex.

Today, right now, some hip parents are bringing up their children to love their bodies and to enjoy sex. Some day these tots will grow into sexually fulfilled adults. Meanwhile all of us inhibited girls in our twenties, thirties, and forties are stumbling along with our guilt feelings, repressions, and a long string of neurotic aversions. It's not our fault—we grew up in the shadow of a dated shame about sex. And fortunately, our inhibitions aren't terminal. We needn't spend our sexually active years suffering from old hangups. The first step toward shedding inhibitions is to recognize which ones we have. Here's a list of the common types:

• *The Nudity Fear.* You can't bear to be bare . . . not in *front* of another human being. You undress in closets, lock bathroom doors, jump when someone catches you wearing a slip, can only make love in the dark.

page 25

• *The Passivity Syndrome.* What, *you* move in bed? Unthinkable! Not when you can lie there like a slab of smoked salmon and have all those horrible things *done* to you. What, you go out and approach a man? Be sexually aggressive?

• *The Missionary Straitjacket.* Well, you surrendered for sex . . . it's even okay, as long as he sticks to the one *normal* way. The alternatives? But those are *depraved!*

• *The Virginity Handicap.* You won't have sex until the wedding bells ring, and then . . . "On your mark, in bed, make it!" Of course, you may perform some pretty convoluted premarital acts, but you wouldn't think of letting him "go all the way." Or (second version) you *did* let him go all the way, but now you're lying about it: You must tell everyone that you're still a virgin.

• *The Guilt Complex.* You went to bed and enjoyed yourself! Horrors! So now you feel *guilty* . . . tormented with anxieties. Does he love you? Can he marry you? Does your mother suspect?

• *The Prude Syndrome.* "Dirty" is your favorite word and can be applied to people, words, and things. You seek ways to be offended, are shocked by how many you find: the way people talk, act, dress . . . disgusting!

• *The Orgasmic Block.* Ah, you love the man . . . undulate beside him jubilantly. Everything moves rhythmically, fluidly, until there is a tensing for the final, nerve-tingling release. *But* it seldom happens. You *say* you enjoy sex even though you never come. Come on! You're still blocked from total release, too self-conscious to let your body respond. This is the most common inhibition of all—and the most frustrating . . . like walking five miles to an ice cream parlor only to find it's closed; or climbing Mt. Everest to discover smog blocks the view. Getting there is only *half* the fun; and if the climax doesn't come after several hundred attempts, trying to get there will become a miserable, useless grind.

Of course, you don't have *all* these inhibitions. But most of us have a vestigial trauma or two. Your sex life may be great . . . until the night Irving tries to flip you over backward, at which point you yelp, "Stop that! You're disgusting!" Or the night Max turns on the lights, and you cringe for the covers. Or your mouth may pucker, prunelike, at a party when someone describes the latest avant-garde nude show. Well, Seventies girl, it's time to clean your mental closets, shake out the dust and rummage of years of accumulated semiconscious inhibitions.

Most women have suffered through at least one major inhibition. Cheers, all inhibitions can be fixed! It may take work and a whole new approach, but you *can* do it. Now that you've spotted your particular inhibition, you're halfway toward getting rid of it. The rest of this book will help you unfold like a sexy little flower, and (we promise) you'll become so loving and lovable that those silly inhibitions won't stand a chance!

Alas, some of us may have more serious sexual problems than inhibitions. Some psychological patterns are really damaging to a woman. Society's mystique of man-over-woman can evolve into its sickest form: the degrading love affair. How can you tell if your love life is normal or slipping into a destructive pattern? Take this quiz.

You may be having Sick Sex if you:
- hate a man after you sleep with him.
- have lots of sex, no satisfaction.
- never make love with the same man twice.
- get depressed after each sexual experience.
- pick lovers you wouldn't bring home to meet your parents.
- find you can't end relationships even when you know you should.
- feel that certain men have a "hold" on you.
- feel inferior to your lovers.
- want to be in complete control of your affair.
- aren't happy unless your lover is begging for love.
- are afraid to tell your analyst about your experiences.
- keep a secret diary, in code, of your adventures.
- look for men in dangerous places . . . the waterfront, deserted parks.
- like to feel you're really a little girl.

If you answered "yes" to *any* of the quiz questions, think about going to an analyst, counselor, or at least your family doctor. *You need professional advice and help.*

Your love affairs should be the most zesty fun you'll ever have—not one miserable crying jag after another. The girl who continually falls in love with the "wrong" man is punishing herself. Psychiatrists diagnose the neurotic "loser" as a chronic masochist. (See Chapter Twelve.) The roots may lie deep in her subconscious, or perhaps in an ugly incident in her life: a rape that aroused her "in spite of herself," an incestuous sex interest. All incidents of that kind intensify guilt feelings over sex.

We think most of you readers are not in such dire straits. But it's always good to know the symptoms of a sick sex life. Even normal girls can sometimes be trapped into a tragically destructive affair. (He was gorgeous, how did you know that you were only 345th in line for his affections?)

Alas, there are many men perfectly capable of hurting a nice girl like you—because the males in this country have long been trained as male chauvinists *extraordinaire*. Many could teach Don Juan a few tricks. We'll show *you* how to avoid dangerous men later on. Meanwhile, the cultural-sexual slack is being taken up, and more men are becoming liberated from their "conquering" role every day. Men and women are becoming better *friends* as well as better lovers. Be glad you are living *today*, Seventies girl. We're bridging the sex gap here and now.

*W*e won't mince words when we explain how your man's naked body works . . . before, during, and after he's made love with you. We'll introduce you to your *own* nude body. How well do you know it? Have you ever seen your fanny in motion? Do you know how to move sensuously in the nude? What are the most erotic ways to caress your breasts? Can you arouse yourself sexually now? We think that's a *must*. And we have many ingenious tricks to turn you on . . . so you can turn *him* on.

During sex itself, do you know how your vagina and clitoris function, how to work the crucial muscles? Can you focus on the red-hot impulses surging from your genitals? We know the secrets . . . and share them.

Most girls have enough sexual insecurity without getting stuck with a poor lover. We'll tell you how to spot the dummies a mile away . . . the ten commonest mistakes any man could make in your bed . . . why a man will never feel exactly as you do during sex.

While we steer you toward good lovers, we'll show you how to make them want you, *madly*. Do you know you can transmit sexy vibrations into everything around you? You'll learn how to handle your sex appeal discreetly, carry on a conversation that says *more*, keep your appearance erotic, but still tasteful.

*M*any girls fall apart on that first night with a new man. Trauma *can* be avoided. We'll tell you how to cope with roommates, relatives, cats, dogs, convertible sofas, and other pitfalls of love. We'll help you lose your virginity without losing your cool.

Over long-term relationships, most women feel they lose ground. How do you keep a man's lust and your own? How much sex can you hope for? How do you manage sex in the morning, in cars, outdoors? Once *you've* learned to be stimulating, shouldn't *he,* too? Can you "fix" a weak lover without hurting his feelings? How do you tell him what you like in bed without sounding authoritarian?

We know the secrets, tricks, and techniques. Benefit from our knowledge, garnered from the ancient love manuals of India, the scientific know-how of the supermodern sex labs, and the experiences of many women. Come with us, and your only sex problem may be how to fight off the extra men!

*The
erotic
senses*

Did you know you have your own special taste? Yes, your skin tastes like no one else's. And your fragrance . . . it's a personal perfume. Even the sounds you make in bed are singular. Ironically, *you* never have much awareness of your own smell and taste during the act of love, because the nature of these perceptions is such that your aura *engulfs* your lover, while his wafts over you. *He* knows the fragrance of your hair, the taste of your lips, the feel of your breasts against his chest, your special love scent.

During sex, *you're* bombarded by your lover's emanations . . . myriad stimuli titillate and tingle your nerves . . . you're lost in *his* touch, smell, taste, and sound. Relish his warm breath, the feel of his smooth thighs, or the calloused palm of his hand over your breast. Watch his excitement grow, from the classic hardening of his desire to the warm flush on his face and chest. (Yes, the darling will actually turn colors.) You'll taste and smell his lips, his skin . . . hear his soft words that eventually fade into equally endearing and exciting gasps. You'll *feel* his growing excitement, the stiffening of his muscles, the anxious, aching thrusts of him . . . and finally, his sweet, damp satisfaction. Bliss!

Through all this lovemaking your senses are totally alert. Every nerve ending reacts as you caress each other with the friction that makes your insides quiver . . . and delicious tension releases in an explosion of ec-stasy. If you are consciously aware of how the erotic senses operate, you can savor those sensations even more. Your erotic senses, along with your life-support systems, are part of your *animal* response pattern, and *crucial* to life. Use sexual function or lose it. The sexual hormones that flow during excitement also keep your body tuned up—moist vagina, firm breasts. Unused vaginas *atrophy!*

Touch

Of your five senses (you know—taste, sight, smell, hearing, and touch), touch is the most intimate and powerful. The impressions made by this fifth sense (your mother's nursing you, your own lovemaking) reach right into your subconscious and stay there . . . and *stay* there. Just shut your eyes and try to recall a powerful experience from your past (you must have had *some*)—a particularly ecstatic (or revolting) lovemaking session, say. What do you recall most vividly? The gleam in his eyes? Probably not. The scent of his aftershave? Well, it may have been nice . . . but no. The *feel* of his skin, the *pressure* of his body, is what you remember most! The way he caressed or thrust, stroked or shoved. The experience was *tactile,* and so is your *memory* of it. And nonsexual tactile experiences are just as potent on recollection: The touch of a soft blanket can evoke cuddly dreams of babyhood, of mother's breast, of everything reassuring.

Because the sense of touch makes such deep inroads into your mind, it is not surprising that actual physical touching is the best way to break down barriers between people. The handshake is the socially acceptable way for people to bridge the communication gap. As a human being, you're a much more physical creature than you may ever have realized: You need the contact of flesh with flesh before any other relationship can form. As the noted psychoanalyst-author Bruno Bettelheim says, "The ability to experience touch as pleasant must precede any human relation." Former President Lyndon B. Johnson (a great hugger) phrased the same sentiment this way: "I must feel a man's skin to know him."

*T*ouch communication, though, is not just a preoccupation of politicians or naked sunbathers at Big Sur encounter groups. *You* do it every day! You may be scratching your head right now, or leaning against a man as you read this book. You touch yourself all day long—and yes, this is a form of communication. You say *I like myself* when you smooth on body lotion, or *I hate myself* when you pick at a pimple. In a typical day you probably spend at least an hour "grooming" yourself—it's a vital part of your life. (The English zoologist and author of *The Naked Ape,* Desmond Morris, contends that all primates thrive mentally on being cleaned and smoothed down.) You carry over your grooming to include your clothes and apartment, brushing lint off that black dress, plumping the pillows. All this physical contact with your belongings can be as reassuring to you as fixing your eye makeup, and the objects themselves can give you *tactile* pleasure. (Love to run your fingers over that suede skirt, right?)

But the most crucial touch communication you engage in involves other people. Just think how many men and women you contact in a day! You may start out being shoved by strangers in a subway, or pressing against them in an elevator. (I assume it's a *crowded* elevator.) Then perhaps you go through repeated "greeting" touches—shaking hands with strangers, hugging your friends, and so on. If you're involved in a nasty affair, you may even slap or push your lover. In more contented moods, you pet, pat, stroke, or tickle the "object of your affections." At night you may sleep away the long hours lying close and warm beside the man you love (or a stand-in: someone you merely find attractive, or a reliable old Teddy bear, or your pet cat). Not to touch would be not to live. You spend your whole life reaching out for people, animals, and objects that delight you—and cringing from those that repel you.

Scientists are just now beginning to understand the power of touch, but for the past twenty years its evidence has been as direct as a pointing finger. You need touch to live—not only in the emotional sense, but in the most real physical way. If no one ever touched you, you would have died or would today be terribly stunted! (I'm not kidding! I'll tell you more about touch deprivation in a moment.)

*T*his is the way the power of touch works: The whole of you is covered by your biggest sensory organ, skin. You probably never give it much thought, but your "birthday suit" is a marvelous piece of equipment. It keeps you warm, covers all your sloshing internal organs, stores fat (you need *some* to survive!), excretes waste, and sends millions of little memos to your brain. You could almost say that the nerves in your skin are like the cells of a battery: They have to be charged (touched) so that your brain can operate (much like a motor). From the tips of your toes to the thin flesh on your scalp you're covered with thousands of *receptors*—little nerve endings that pick up information and zing it along up to your brain.

If you're attuned to your skin's amazing sensory properties, you can pick up some fantastic data. Edward Hall, a Northwestern University anthropologist, maintains that a girl can feel heat radiating from a sexually aroused (or angry) male standing *three feet* away! He also says you can tell a good party from a bad one *through your skin*. (Clue: the good parties feel warm because of the excitement they generate.) All these perceptions are reactions to *thermal* touch—the feel of someone's temperature—which normally precedes actual physical touch. Some fastidious folks are so sensitive about even *thermal* touch that they won't sit in a chair that's still warm from another person's body.

All this association seems less mystifying if you understand that the skin is made up, in part, of the *ectoderm* (outermost of the three layers of your embryo material), and that your eyes and other sense organs are also covered by this ectoderm, and so there is a perceptual and intense relationship throughout your entire nervous system. It is this relationship that enabled the late Helen Keller, blind and deaf from birth, to discover the entire world through touch on the tender palms of her hands. And because the impressions of touch imprint so strongly on the brain, many children who cannot learn to read visually can do so by the Montessori method, which involves feeling sandpaper cutout letters.

We can learn much through our skin. (Perhaps only a Helen Keller ever fully realizes *how much*.) And whether we're aware of it or not, skin *stimulation* does trigger even the most elementary functions inside every living, breathing animal. Take dogs, for example. Have you ever watched a bitch with her newborn pups? She starts *licking* her babies just as fast as she can deliver them. For years this syndrome was thought to be a "washing" process, but recent studies of mammals at the Cornell (University) Behavior Farm proved the newborn *had* to be licked in order to have their genito-urinary and nervous systems activated. Baby lambs that were not licked couldn't stand up; many even died.

The most startling evidence of the magical power of touch was turned in by Seymour Levine, an associate professor of psychiatry at the Stanford University School of Medicine, who in the 1960's proved that even painful shocks were better for baby rats than no contact at all! Levine used three groups of rats to prove his theory. One group was raised by its mother in the usual cuddly litter. The second was isolated completely (but given food, of course). The third poor little group was subjected to a series of electric shocks. Who were the losers? As you might expect, the unhandled baby rats were stunted and weak, had no control over their urination, and were nervous wrecks. But the big surprise was that the rats who received electric shocks were just as sassy as their cuddled and coddled counterparts.

Well, if skin stimulation can work such wonders for lambs, puppies, and baby rats, what might it have done for *you* when you were a baby? The answer: everything! As with four-legged animals, touch is the razor's edge between life and death for the infant *human* being, too. Dr. René Spitz, a child psychiatrist connected with the University of Colorado School of Medicine, proved the importance of skin stimulation among humans when some fifteen years ago he toured orphanages that were raising babies without fondling them. The infants were given food and kept clean, but because of a shortage of nurses, were left to lie, untouched, in their cribs. The horrible result: The children became little lumps of apathy. They were mentally slow, poorly coordinated, and many just withered away until they *died!*

𝒩ow, how does all this infant research relate to *you*—a grown-up who, let's say, was *not* ignored in babyhood but rather held, rocked, stroked, by a doting mother? Well, have you ever noticed that when a man strokes your cheek, you automatically kiss his fingertips? Try it; it's true (and fun). But alas, you're not being terribly romantic and cute; you're betraying a throwback to early infancy. That's right—you were born with an instinct to respond to a touch on your cheek by making a sucking motion with your lips. That motion was nature's clue to your mother that you wanted her nipple and the warm flow of milk that would follow.

Later, your social conditioning taught you which types of touch were socially acceptable. The interesting thing here is the variation in acceptability: Every society has its own touch code! If you were an Arabian maiden or Italian mamma, you'd be getting more kisses, hugs, pats, and pushes than if you're what I think you are—a touch-starved American girl. But don't feel too bad; most of us are.

Edward Hall, the anthropologist I mentioned earlier, described the different national attitudes toward touch in his book *The Hidden Dimension.* Americans rate low on his list of touching cultures. He says we go through life insulated by our cars and machines, that most of our social habits widen the distance between us as individuals instead of bringing us closer together. We're taught to hold ourselves in, to avoid contact if possible. Don't you say "Excuse me" if you accidentally brush up against someone? Even within a family there may not be much physical contact. American mothers *rarely* breast-feed their babies and almost never carry them around physically. In primitive societies children are *carried* by the mother, not pushed ahead in a stroller.

Hall mentions several cultures that hold strikingly different attitudes toward touching. Arabs stand very close to one another during casual conversations and (gasp!) don't even mind feeling other people's breath on their faces. The typical Japanese family revels in touch—at night everyone curls up around a hibachi stove and plays "footsie." Eskimo families sleep together under a communal fur blanket (or at least they used to; now that they're Americans, what was good enough for Nanook of the North may today be passé). The French, Italians, and other Southern Europeans touch one another more than we do. And Russian and Latin Americans are also openly tactile.

Sidney Jourard, a Florida University psychologist, is another behavioral researcher who conducted his own study of the touch differences among nations of the world and came up with some startling impressions. He observed couples sitting at café tables in four different cities and counted how many times each touched. In Paris, the average couple came into physical contact 110 times during an hour (and they were just having a conversation!) The action in San Juan, Puerto Rico, was even more exciting: The Puerto Rican couples patted, tickled, and caressed 180 times during the same amount of time. But in London, the typical British couple never touched at all. And back home in the U.S., the Americans did little better—just one pat or two during an hour's conversation.

Of course, right here in America we do indulge in some *formalized* touching. The Presidential candidate doesn't shake thousands of hands for naught; he knows that simple warm handclasp can get him a vote. Why? The reason isn't logical, it's visceral. That old longing for the warmth and security of physical contact makes a handshake a good way to cross the invisible barrier between strangers. Shaking hands is (1) an offer of friendship, (2) saying "I like you" or "I accept you," and (3) assuring the other fellow that you don't find him repulsive. The last may seem redundant, but if anyone has ever cringed when you came close to him, you know the traumatic hurt that *not* touching can inflict. The worst insult in our society is to refuse a proffered hand. The greatest compliment: to offer it.

When the handshake is extended to hand-holding, you're saying that your acquaintanceship is not fleeting: "We're good friends" or "We're mother and daughter" or "We're sweethearts." You can *tell* a lot from hand-holding: The nervous person's palm is clammy, the excited person's is hot, the disinterested's is cool. The hand you *want* to hold is warm, just lightly moist (to show he's interested!)

A more exuberant form of touch is the hug, a gesture reserved for people you know very well. (You *can* hug someone when you're introduced for the first time, but he'll probably be stunned and back off.) It's a great way to let a good friend know he (or she) is special. The hug is an abbreviated embrace—a way of saying, "I'm *really, really* glad to see you!" You can also hug friends at dramatic moments to show you're really happy for them. ("That's wonderful you're getting married"—hug . . . hug.)

While you're in there close, it might be great to plant a kiss somewhere (on the cheek, say). This adds intimacy to the greeting—like saying, "You're *superspecial!*" If the kissed person wipes his cheek afterward, watch out! But I think you'll find that most people *love* to be kissed!

Human beings open up like buds after even that slight an intimacy. It's the old emotional need for contact. Don't you like the friends who kiss and hug you *more* than those who don't? Sure you do, and the reason is, you feel more secure and better liked by a person with whom you've had physical contact.

*T*ouch *will* bring you closer (physically and emotionally) to other people. So loosen up, warm up, touch more, try *not* to shrink back. Most important, don't wait for people to approach *you*. The power of touch lies in its being generously proffered; be the first to offer contact and you'll not often be rejected. Throw your arms around someone—for real impact. Be the first to hold out a hand. Give a quick hug and kiss to the friends you know well, and you'll get to know them a lot better. I've tried this system. It *works*. The best, most comfortable get-togethers usually begin with a nice touch-and-kiss greeting. Touch, after all, is the most *intimate* of the senses. Use it to your advantage! It isn't enough to look, sound, and smell—even *taste*—nice. The most powerful impressions you make will be by touch.

And remember, how you react tactilely in your social life is vital to your sex life. There may be a girl somewhere who winces when a man holds her hand, yet still is able to glue herself to him in bed—but she's a freak. The rule is: The less inhibited you are about touching and kissing in a social setting, the more fun you'll have in bed. The *best* lovers are those who are *extremely* tactile. They *adore* the feel of other people's bodies and aren't ashamed of their own. And the girl who likes to explore with her fingers and press her whole being against her lover will have more fun than the woman who lies there as limp as last summer's air mattress.

*T*he really sensual man or woman savors the changing temperatures and textures of the flesh during lovemaking. And there *are* changes. As Masters and Johnson, those by-now venerable specialists on human sex, tell us, frigid women—women who *dislike* sex, not just those who don't have orgasms—are actually physically *cold:* Their bodies maintain a lower temperature, and their skin contracts. The sexually aroused male or female is much *hotter*.

During sex, touch plays its most intrusive role—literally; penetration is the deepest intimate contact you'll ever experience. Male and female bodies "fit" together. To get closer, closer, closer, until the two of you (as they say) become one is not only a nerve-zinging sensual treat, but also a rewarding emotional experience. And it's a general rule that the more two people care for each other, the more they'll touch before, during, and after making love.

If *your* tastes run to lots of physical affection in bed, you no doubt know a lot about what sex manuals unfortunately call "foreplay." (It really is *total* play that shouldn't be restricted to one rigid "phase" of lovemaking. More about *that* in Chapter Nine.) The literature on the subject is voluminous. Dr. Havelock Ellis, that grand old daddy of sexologists, has written chapters on the caressing of the male organ alone—not to mention all the other marvelous, delicious tactile advances you can enchant your lover with. Ellis's basic message, of course: Touch, touch, touch!

Smell
Next to touch, smell may well be the most active erotic sense. In lower mammals (like dogs and cats), smell may be the whole courtship. Male dogs sniff a bitch to see if she's in heat, and act accordingly. Odors don't influence us quite *that* much . . . but *more* than you would guess.

Did you know that the Eskimos aren't really rubbing noses when they kiss? They're *smelling* each other's faces, a sign of deep affection and attraction. Eskimos are fully aware of what *we* may have missed—that each person has a unique aroma. When they like someone, they move physically closer together immediately.

Without really thinking about it, we tend to associate smell strongly with our lovers. After a long separation you may be quite overcome on sensing again that indescribable aroma that means "John, love, closeness, bed, sex" all at once. It's comfort even to smell the clothes of an absent lover.

In America, concentration on smell is mainly aimed at spraying it out of existence. Aerosol bombs are blasted at armpits, vaginas . . . now even penises get a jet of spiced scent. In Europe, smells are allowed to "ripen" on the body. Continental lovers expect stronger odors that might overwhelm a deodorized American.

Certainly, odors *do* have an aphrodisiac effect. Sweat, vaginal lubrication, and other body secretions can chemically arouse desire in either sex . . . *if* there is no prejudice against them. Since most people in this country *are* biased against body odors, we suggest you keep them down . . . except with visiting European lovers. Even a clean, deodorized body works up quite a scent during ardorous amours. So there *will* be something for the olfactories to sniff!

Let your personal preference (and your lover's) be your guide. Some women enjoy the smell of a man's perspiration (if it isn't a week old). If you know that turns you on, grab your man before he gets under the shower. Catch him after his morning jog, or surprise him by slipping under him while he's doing push-ups. Likewise, some men really savor a slightly gamey girl (at least an undeodorized one). The youth culture in general is said to emanate "groovy smells." Dyan Cannon, after an Esalen bout, addressed her group of co-guests and said, "I dig your smells."

At any rate, you should not be so mentholated or chlorined or cologned that your own true aroma can't seep through. Your individual scent is one of the strongest holds you can exert on a man's erotic memory. One girl we know was deeply touched when her absent lover mailed her a eucalyptus leaf. "I never smelled one until now," he wrote, "but when I held the leaf to my nose, I suddenly recalled your body . . . making love to you. This is the closest I've ever come to your own special scent. I miss you." Lovely man!

Taste
Taste and smell are so closely woven that it is hard to tear the two apart. How can you separate the taste of salty water from the smell of brine? Your tongue is one of your most acute sex organs. That pink, nubby tip of flesh is covered with tingly nerve endings. It's so sensitive, in fact, that it possesses some of the erectile properties of the clitoris! Point your tongue and see! Use your pink, probing tongue to taste your lover wherever you want . . . and to lick him, too. Your tongue also serves your sense of *touch:* As it caresses your lover, it receives deep stimulation itself.

*T*he taste of vaginal lubricants is actually erotic to a male who wants to taste them. Closely associated with the dense sexual musk of this area, the genital kiss rewards both he who administers and she who receives. And you *can* kiss your man's genitals, too. Many girls enjoy the velvety smoothness of the penis, the delicate moist slit at its tip.

Oral sex seems to be on the rise in our culture. It can be an incredibly delicious, delicate experience. Many girls who cannot climax during genital sex find that they can climax while their lover kisses their clitoris and vagina. (The stimulation is obviously more concentrated.)

At any rate, the female-hygiene industry is invading this territory of sexual union as well, by promoting raspberry- and cherry-flavored douches to add an extra fillip to oral sex. The manufacturers won't admit that, of course, but why raspberry—unless *someone* is tasting? It's an extra, if artificial, refinement, so you'd best be sure your man likes those flavors! (And if he does, why not *fresh* fruit squeezed onto your body, instead of a factory-made substitute?) Many men like their girls' natural taste, which they say is distinctive. Some unabashed lovers we know compared their lady-loves to "honey," "vanilla," "pear nectar," "ripe peaches."

Sound

As all the senses interlock during intense sexual excitement, sounds also play an erotic role. Sex is not quiet. There are pats, laughs, moans, groans, sighs, sobs, and indefinable creaks and squeaks. African tribesmen long ago recognized the most erotic sound of all—the squishing of the penis in a moist vagina. As part of a young African tribesman's initiation into manhood, he was stationed outside a hut and told to listen to the sounds from within (*squish, squish*). The noise was really only a stick in a mud hole, but if the youth thought he was hearing a couple mating, he got ten points and was definitely grown-up!

The Hindus developed a whole art of love sounds. The *Kama Sutra* details appreciative noises a woman was *supposed* to emit while making love —a repertoire of love sounds. Most of these express pleasurable anguish. They sound unlikely to the Western ear—"hinn," "coo," "phoutt," "phatt," "souatt," and "platt."

You can enjoy both words and inarticulate love sounds in your own amours. Calling your lover's name is a word-caress. Whispering an encouragement—"You are filling me . . . come deeper . . . deeper . . ."—can drive a man wild with passion and add to your own excitement, too. Most couples speak during sex, to compliment each other's bodies and sensuous motions. Think about what words you'd like him to say to you; now say them out loud to yourself . . . and to him the next time you are making love.

Panting also sounds erotic and combines with the hot rush of breath against the lover's chest or face for a double stimulus. If you're really excited, it isn't easy to control these erotic sounds. And why would you want to? He'll adore them!

Sight

Sexologists have long attributed sight as an *erotic* sense almost exclusively to males. Doctors studying pupilometrics have found that men's pupils dilate at the sight of nude photographs. Some men will have an erection if they see a nude woman, or even glimpse deep cleavage or bare thigh. Hence the popularity of "feelthy" pictures and blue movies.

The first studies indicated that women weren't much turned on by the sight of the male nude. But now a reappraisal may be in order. Some of this disinterest could be caused by social conditioning. It's always been fine for men to ogle, but unthinkable for a woman to have pinups of bikini-clad men. Women's lib may score in this sexual battle, for women are *looking* more now and enjoying it! Certainly many women are aroused by the sight of their naked lover. His whole form and his genitals are beautiful . . . and tantalizing.

In any case, during lovemaking there is a good deal to look at. Colors heighten, the flesh blushes redder as excitement mounts. Everyone responds to red with eagerness and interest (a fact not overlooked by opportunistic packagers). The reddening of your lips, chest, and (if he's looking that way) vaginal area swells the man's excitement. And as the blood pours into his genitals and you see his flesh color, your passion increases as well.

Visual expressions on lovers' faces are also stimulating. The face contorts with excitement. Your lover looks down, his features almost unrecognizable as the tension of climax approaches. This should please you, the woman who has driven him to such passion. And your head thrown back, mouth open to a soft "oh" . . . many men say there is nothing so beautiful as a woman's face during orgasm; since he made it possible, it stimulates and fulfills him as well.

To quote the sensual, erotic Indian love manual, the *Kama Sutra:*
> The face of a woman should be her mirror to pleasure
> The man should read there her desire and will.

The more your senses develop, the more pleasure they will give you. Our society has not encouraged much touch stimulation until very, very recently. You have so much *potential* that hasn't been tapped (literally!) . . . it's almost as if you're under the influence of novocaine, numbed by the effects of a touchless culture.

Even if you are an ardent lover or masturbator, your senses can benefit from *more* stimulation. Take these titillating touch tests and see! Some tests may not *seem* sexual, but they all *will* prepare those tender nerve endings for your ultimate super sexual bliss.

In total blackness:
- Soak in a hot bath.
- Take a needle-sharp cool shower.

- Rub yourself dry with rough towels.
- Put on a satin gown.

Lights on. Now collect:
- piece of fur
- suede fabric
- kid gloves
- panne velvet
- ostrich feather
- a powder puff
- pearls
- polished wooden bowl
- fresh ferns
- flower petals
- lace panties
- or other "touchables"

Tie a scarf over your eyes as a blindfold. Now fondle each item—*individually*—for at least ten minutes. Use the tenderest tips of your fingers . . . stroke the item lightly. Later, grasp it more firmly, feel it grow warm in your palm. Slowly touch different parts of your body with each item, paying attention to your responses. Concentrate on the textures you feel. The cool, bruised flesh of flower petals . . . the hard creaminess of pearls . . . the silkiness of hand-rubbed wood . . . and so on.

Don't be afraid to try coarser textures. Anything that perks up the nerve endings will help you respond ecstatically to touches of other kinds (like your lover's caresses). In fact, it's fun to try these contrast exercises (touch one object, then the other):

Contrast: The Smooth and the Rough
- a rough stone . . . and a piece of absorbent cotton
- burlap cloth . . . and a lettuce leaf
- a nail file . . . and a silk ribbon

Contrast: The Hot and the Cold
- an ice cube . . . and a warm candle
- a spoon . . . and a warm, boiled egg
- a crystal glass . . . and a rubber hot-water bottle

Take outdoor touch tests, too (but with your eyes open!)
- Roll over in spring grass.
- Dive into a cool lake.

- Touch snow—and taste it.
- Lie down on a sun-warmed rock.
- Let hot sand trickle through your fingers.

Scandinavians throw themselves into sensual pleasure. Try some of their pursuits as part of your touch testing:
- Take a hot sauna, follow by a cold shower.
- Swim in a heated pool, roll in fresh snow afterward.
- Eat hot cheese fondue outdoors on a cold day.
- Ski down a trail, then drink hot buttered rum.

Touch Games
- Crawl into bed nude. Pull covers over your head. Stay in your self-made "tent" for at least a half hour. Feel your body heat wrap around you. Enjoy the soft fuzz of the blanket, the smooth warmth of the sheets.
- Take hot sheets from clothes dryer and wrap your naked self in them. Alternative: Place huge towels over radiator. When towels are hot, wrap them around you.
- Put on a long nylon nightgown and wear it into the shower. Watch it stick to your skin as water pours over you. Shut your eyes, think about something physically provocative.
- Crawl over the floor of your apartment. On your hands and knees, explore every surface—shag rugs, polished parquet, slick linoleum, tile floors.
- Naked, slip on your winter coat. Shut your eyes and concentrate on the feel of the coat lining, the weight of the coat upon your body; feel the delicate pricks from the millions of tiny hairs.
- Sit on top of a running dishwasher, clothes washer, or other hot, vibrating appliance (like a turned-on stereo speaker). Feel the concentrated impulses traveling through your body. Unromantic, but tingly.

Smell Adventures
- Open every spice bottle you own, and blindfolded, try to identify the herbs.
- Ask the florist for the duskiest rose, sniff it all the way home.
- Bury your nose in freshly laundered sheets.
- Sniff a pot of simmering stew, or onions sautéeing in a pan of golden butter.

- Inhale the aroma of clothes after wearing.
- Keep an orange studded with cloves in your closet.
- Go to bed in darkness—with incense burning.
- Try scented candles, or drop some of your favorite perfume on a light bulb.
- Nuzzle your pet cat or dog after you've bathed.
- Hold a baby, smell its skin.
- Use lemon juice in your hair rinse.
- Spray perfume on your pillowcases (or your lover's pillowcase).
- Burn peat in a fireplace, twigs from a pine tree.
- Walk in a forest, collect pinecones.
- Lie in a fresh sunny meadow, eyes shut, and try to identify grass or hay scents.
- Smell a crackling fire, a charcoal hibachi.
- Go into a Japanese shop, a Chinese restaurant, a Hungarian spice store, an Armenian grocery . . . learn the different special smells each has.
- Try to isolate the smells in different rooms of your apartment: curry in the kitchen? soap and bath powder in the bathroom? cologne and air-conditioner-filtered air in the bedroom? leather and book mustiness near the bookshelves?

Taste treats
- Lick a frozen custard as slowly as possible.
- Eat Chinese or Japanese foods with chopsticks.
- Munch fried chicken with your fingers and lick them.
- Hold a piece of Swiss chocolate in your mouth until it melts.
- Swirl a good wine or brandy in your mouth before swallowing it.
- Crunch a vegetable you don't usually have raw—carrot, green pepper, onion, corn.
- Drink soup from a cup.
- Eat fifteen perfect raspberries, one by one.
- Go to a cheese store and taste ten new varieties.
- Visit an ethnic restaurant you've never tried.
- Hold a blade of new grass in your teeth.
- Drink the milk straight from a coconut.
- Eat an entire meal in blackness.
- Alone, blow soap bubbles.
- Alone, chew bubble gum, try for a giant pink balloon.

Sensual sights

- Go to a museum and study male nude statues and paintings.
- Visit the beach, look at real seminude men.
- Shut your eyes, try to recall every visual detail of your lover's body.
- Look at your man's clothing when he's not in it.
- Watch an ocean tide flow in, ebb out.
- Step in footprints on the sand.
- Watch a sun rise.
- Go to a track and watch the men run.
- In the mountains, go out at midnight to look for stars and constellations.
- As dusk falls, watch shadows creep into your apartment.
- Spend a rainy day at the window.
- Be the first outside on a snowy morning.
- Watch a cat nurse her newborn kittens.
- Study a candle as it burns down.
- Look at an antique watch or clock as it ticks.
- See how many textures you are wearing—silk, wool, nylon.
- Count the colors on your body—brown for hair, blue for eyes, rose for nipples, white for teeth.
- Wash your face clean, naked-clean, and study it in a hand mirror for half an hour.

All these sense exercises and touch games have something to do with sex. Do them! They will put you in "touch" with yourself and your world. Every time you are stimulated, a synapse (connection in the nervous system) is formed, honing the erotic reactions to a fine edge. You are bodily prepared, psychologically receptive to the lightest touch, the most covert glance, the whiff of love-scent, the sound of an interested man's voice. You will be as keen as a doe in the forest, every nerve alert, aware.

When you do fall warmly, happily into bed, all those lovely synapses will be waiting . . . and the sexual stimulation will charge right through your toned-up, tuned-up body. The Masters and Johnson experiments in orgasm indicated that the more accustomed a woman is to stimulation, the less time she will require to reach orgasm. That means you will be less likely to fall prey to one common sex malady: Man climaxes when woman is just beginning to be aroused. Easy to arouse, you will be glorious to satisfy!

page 47

Know
your body
. . . nude

FOUR

$\mathcal{D}$o you know how your back looks naked? If you have a full-length mirror, stand in front of it nude, holding a small mirror in your hand. Now slowly turn your body, using the hand mirror to reflect all aspects of you. If you don't own a full-length mirror (do buy one immediately), stand naked in the fitting room of a department store (preferably one where the sales force isn't oversolicitous!) Face yourself, without the disguise of clothes. See yourself as lovers will see you.

Too many girls don't know their own naked bodies. Mrs. Deborah Szekely, a West Coast obesity expert, cures fat teen-age girls of their compulsive eating habits by forcing them to stare at their nude reflections. "These girls had eaten their way up to four hundred pounds or even more," Mrs. Szekely explains, "and they were able to let it happen because they were out of communication with their own bodies!" When the girls faced corporal reality, they were able to diet.

You may not weigh four hundred pounds (we hope you don't!), but you still may be a stranger to your true physical self. Take this test and see:

How well do you know your naked body?
- Have you ever seen your behind in *motion?*
- How many birthmarks or moles do you have?
- Do the veins at the back of your knee show?
- Are your buttocks pocked with stretch marks?
- Are the soles of your feet calloused?
- Have you felt your clitoris?
- Are your nipples pink, or brownish?
- Do you have hairs around your nipples?

- Is your back freckled?
- Are your breasts pointy, round, or droopy in *profile?*

If you haven't answered every question *without* hesitation, take this time to get acquainted with yourself in the nude. Yes, right now! Shuck your clothes. Now, confront your mirror image. Turn and catch the rear view. Now walk. Jog in place. Sit. Squat. Skip. Jump. Lie down. Bend over . . . and keep looking.

Watch yourself naked in every conceivable pose. Surprising, isn't it? Who would have guessed that your behind *jiggled* like that? Or that your breasts looked so supple when you lean back? Everyone is different, of course, and you will find some very *unique* things about your own precious body. Love your body, and preen. You're luscious and special.

Discovery games to play in the nude
- Count your birthmarks.
- Fill a bowl with body lotion, smooth it over *every* exposed inch of you.
- Sit cross-legged, massage your toes.
- Spend an entire day without clothing, at *home*, of course!
- Call someone you love on the phone, watch your naked body as you talk.
- Open a window (if it isn't winter), let the wind blow on your breasts.
- Lie in bed for two hours (not reading—just daydreaming).
- Curl up on a rug and drink champagne.
- Lie in a bubble bath for an hour.
- Do a handstand against a wall.
- Perform thirty minutes of hearty calisthenics.

These games can become lessons, as you learn how your flesh responds to different stimuli. We won't give you *all* the answers, but be sure to notice how temperatures and emotions change the very texture of your skin. When you're warm, your skin will feel moist, the tissues will be flaccid. Cold reverses these symptoms: You'll turn to gooseflesh, your nipples will stiffen. During the phone conversation or daydream, you will see how your emotions influence your skin—texture, moistness, and temperature will be fluctuating with every thought you express or every fantasy you entertain. Even the color of your skin changes . . . watch carefully and enjoy your own variety!

Your uncovered self is the *real* you . . . the essence of your sensuality, your femaleness. Think of yourself as a magnificent being, every undulating physical part of you. All the pleasure and powerful sensation that you feel stems from your *humanity*—the fact that you are a *female, human,* warm-blooded mammal. Yes, you have a mind, and you should develop it as well—but the brain works best in a healthy, pulsating body. Don't intellectualize yourself out of your hot-blooded joy. Adore your body. Even if it isn't perfect (whose is?), it's yours—the *only* one you'll ever have (unless you believe in reincarnation; and even then, you may come back as a *horse*). Treasure your breasts, bottom, stomach, long legs, and your precious rose-colored center of sexuality—your genitals. To deny any of these is self-destructive. There is *no* part of you that you should fear to look at, touch—or show to a lover. You *must* love yourself before you can love others. And before *they* can love *you*. Feel adorable, and you will be adored!

Your Genitals—Before, During, and After Lovemaking
Here we are—at the source of all your marvelous sexual feelings, buried within you both anatomically *and* psychologically. Most of us don't have a full comprehension of just how we are constructed "down there," what happens to the genitals throughout the sexual cycle. Here is what you need to know about that special part of your body.

There are two words you've probably heard or read frequently—vulva and vagina—and they might confuse you. Simply, the first refers to external female genitals, and the vagina is one of several internal genital organs. The vulva is composed of the wide outer lips called the labia majora, and the two inner minor lips called the labia minora, plus the clitoris, which is the firm, pealike structure, one-quarter to one-half inch in size, located at the point where the two minor lips come together; then comes the entrance to the vagina, located *below* your urinary opening; the urinary outlet itself, located *above* the vaginal opening; and the Bartholin's glands. All of these comprise the vulva.

The vagina itself is a tiny tunnel extending three or four inches toward the cervix; it is a mucous membrane channel, self-lubricating and cleaning, and capable of great elasticity.

Now, look at the diagrams of female genitals on the next two pages. Reread the preceding, and locate each area mentioned on the diagrams. Look at the diagrams again, and touch each part of you that corresponds to the genitals shown.

External Female Genitals

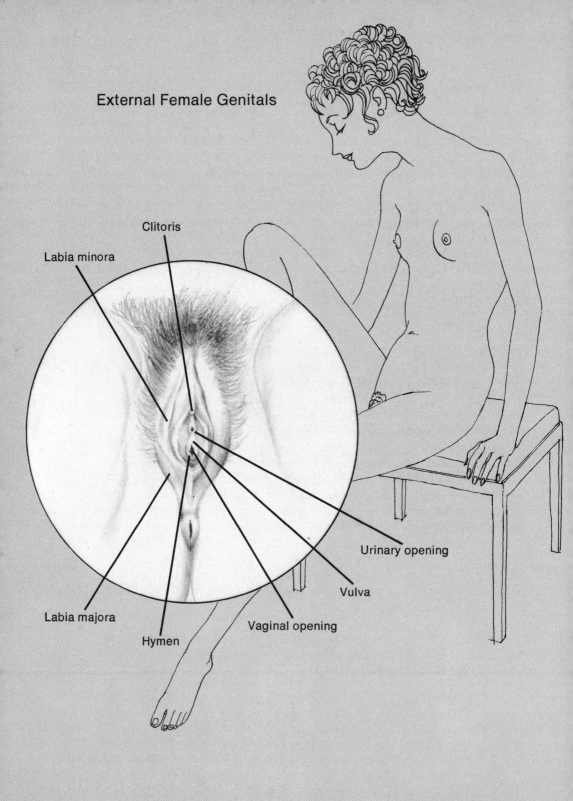

Clitoris

Labia minora

Labia majora

Hymen

Vaginal opening

Vulva

Urinary opening

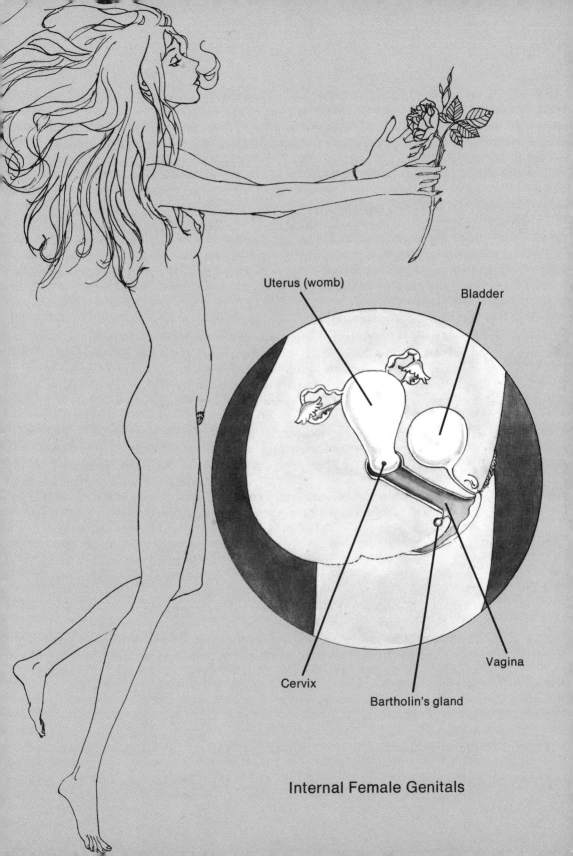

Uterus (womb)

Bladder

Cervix

Bartholin's gland

Vagina

Internal Female Genitals

$\mathcal{N}$ow that you know *where* your genitals are, let's proceed to what they *do*. Start with the labia majora—the larger vaginal lips. As soon as your lover approaches you sexually, your labia majora expand with excitement, and the fold of skin near your vagina lifts away a bit. After sexual activity, when excitement subsides, the labia majora recede to presex condition. If no orgasm occurs, they may stay engorged (swollen) for some time.

Just inside the labia majora are the labia minora—the smaller vaginal lips. These swell to about three times normal size during sexual excitation. They protrude and turn deep pink! Some women's labia become *violently* red when excitement is high and the vaginal area has secreted its lubrication. Afterward, your labia minora pale again. (By the way, no pink color means no possibility of orgasm!)

Next to the labia minora you have two little Bartholin's glands: As you near orgasm, these glands secrete mucus. For a long time, doctors thought this secretion was only to lubricate the vagina and ease the way of the penis. Not so, say Masters and Johnson. The Bartholin's eagerly work for reproduction: Their droplets make your vagina more receptive to sperm by neutralizing the body acid that would destroy them.

The clitoris is your pleasure dome. It is unique in the anatomy of human beings. The male penis (also used for urination) is not *exclusively* a sexual organ, as the clitoris is. But in many ways, your clitoris *is* like a mini-penis—it erects and is your most sensitive sex organ. As soon as you're excited, the clitoris becomes firm, and grows increasingly sensitive and thickened. It is so vulnerable that direct touches on the tip can be painful. When sexual tension is released, the clitoris recedes to normal size and position unless there has been no orgasm. If you're left "high and dry," the clitoris may remain thick and irritated for hours. Doctors have had some difficulty observing this sex organ because it is so tiny and hidden during sexual relations. Masters and Johnson did learn, however, that direct stimulation of the clitoris occurs best when you are above the man or by his side. No wonder women's lib cries, "Out from under!" When you are astride your man, you can control contact between the clitoris and your lover's pelvic area. By moving your body back and forth, making repeated contacts between the clitoris and his penis and body, you speed to climax. Some women have a clitoris that naturally is placed low and in easy contact with the man's body . . . so these girls are swiftly stimulated to climax. In other women, the clitoris is so buried in the labia folds that it cannot easily be titillated. These girls need manual or oral stimulation and in intercourse will prefer the side-by-side or the woman-on-top position. In the conventional man-on-top position, it's awkward for *any* clitoris to receive stimulation.

*T*he vagina is the original tunnel of love. Half a minute (more or less) after you start to become excited, the walls of that channel secrete lubrication (which will allow a man's penis to glide right in without pain or chafing to you). Then the vagina lengthens and widens (this is before a penis enters; when *that* happens, the vagina adjusts to grip it), and its walls turn passionate purple. During orgasm, these purple walls flutter in involuntary contractions—a *status orgasmus* (super orgasm) can be a spastic contraction lasting from twenty to sixty seconds. The maximum average orgasm quivers up to fifteen times . . . all of which can happen in less than five seconds! Then the walls of the vagina collapse, the vagina pales, a glorious warmth begins to spread out from your pelvic area to every part of your body . . . you are at peace. Isn't it marvelous?

You know how your genitals function during sex. Now, hold a magnifying hand mirror and take a good look at your vulva parts in their currently relaxed state. If you've winced at this suggestion, you still have inhibitions. Take that mirror and *look!* How could you not be curious about this precious, lovely part of your body?

Use the diagrams on the previous pages if you want to identify the different areas again. No trouble spotting your clitoris, though, is there? Feel it. Part your vaginal lips and peek inward. Gently poke a finger inside, feel for the knob of flesh at the back of the vaginal tunnel. That's the cervix—entrance to the womb. Note how close your urinary canal is—running parallel to your vagina. Can you feel how elastic your vagina is? Push at the walls.

If you own a diaphragm, you know your basic vaginal size. Many girls worry that their vagina is too big or too small. Remember, it's performance that counts, not size. Note: Vaginas tend to stretch with repeated sex, and much more with childbirth, so your vagina may *seem* to grow wider with the years. But any vagina in good muscular condition adjusts to fit the penis, *any* penis, so everything is snug with proper friction.

*N*ow what about vulval and vaginal odors? As we said earlier, the amount of body odor deemed desirable is up to the two people involved. When starting a new liaison, you may want to be on the safe side and keep your vagina especially clean-smelling. If you don't like the idea of using a vaginal spray, you might just dab some perfume around your pubic area.

(Don't put it *anywhere* on the vulva—burns!) Most men prefer a musky perfume to a sweet one, so leave the flowery, light scents for daylight and girl-friend lunches. For perfume in the nude, use the deeper, heavier scents . . . Quadrille by Balenciaga, Cabochard by Madame Grès, Femme by Marcel Rochas.

Douching is not an everyday part of your hygiene. Too many girls feel obliged to douche after sex. They're wasting time; a douche is *not* a contraceptive. And it's not really needed to clean a healthy vagina, which is actually self-sanitizing. A warm, wet washcloth can easily remove semen or lubricating jellies and creams from the external genitals. Too much douching actually *irritates* vaginal tissues. Even a monthly douche after your period is superfluous.

But don't toss out your douche bag yet. Doctors *do* recommend a douche when you have a minor vaginal infection. The three vaginal conditions most of us will suffer at some time are:
1. itching (caused by emotional upsets or a fungus);
2. inflammation (from infections by bacteria like gonococci);
3. dryness (because of too little secretion).

Most common of all is the minor vaginal infection. The main symptom is a whitish discharge, which may or may not have an odor. It is called leukorrhea—or "the whites"—and is quite normal. The remedy is douching (one tablespoon of white vinegar to two quarts of warm water in a douche bag) two or three times a week until symptoms cease. Then stop douching.

If the discharge causes itching and pain in the vagina and around the vulval area, the cause might be a tiny living organism called a trichomonad. This is also quite common, and its cause is still unknown. The diagnosis must be made by a doctor, who simply takes a smear of the secretion from the vagina and looks at it under a microscope. Treatment is easy and effective, usually given in tablet form to be swallowed.

Another possible cause of an itchy vagina is a fungus called Candida albicans. This discharge can be quite heavy, the itch unbearable. Doctors diagnose this, too, through microscopic examination of the discharge. Treatment includes inserting special tablets high into the vagina over a several-week period, plus an ointment for the vulva. It is also recommended that the lover use the ointment on his penis.

Don't be frightened by any of these conditions. All are relatively common, happen to most women some time in their lives. Important: See your doctor as soon as symptoms appear. Douching can *encourage* some already-started fungus, dry out tissues that are already irritated by lack of secretions. You should know a gynecologist whom you can call to consult about any symptoms that might occur.

On the aesthetic aspects of your vagina, you may want to do something about your pubic hair. Some girls sport a neat Vandyke, others are nearly hairless, and still others nurture an overgrown thatch. If you want a more neatly trimmed garden, use a gentle depilatory, or try a bikini waxing treatment (keeps skin soft and hairless longer), or give yourself a haircut. Keep your pubic hair clean, of course, and if it's long, you might give it a quick brushing. If it's too coarse, use a cream rinse or conditioner in the shower. Many girls have pubic hair that is a different color from their head hair. (Of course dyed blondes show brunette vaginas—but it also happens naturally.) Some men find this provocative.

Breasts: The Second Most Erogenous Zone
In these braless days, breasts are more noticeable than ever before. You probably think about your breasts more . . . and are more conscious of them as they bob freely along within your clothes. Men have always liked breasts (their mother's and yours). And young girls have always fussed and fretted over them.

Did you know that your breasts:
- are really glorified sweat glands?
- extend *anatomically* from the second to the sixth rib, and from the edge of the breastbone to the armpit?
- aren't equal in size? (The left one's usually bigger.)
- can help you attain orgasm?
- get bigger and more sensitive if you take the Pill?

Nature, of course, intended that your breasts be used to suckle babies. You are, after all, a *mammal;* that is, you have mammaries (breasts), which produce milk at the proper time. But Mother Nature, being nice, also thoughtfully turned the breasts into your second most powerful erogenous zone. (You *know* where the first zone is.) The Masters and Johnson study turned up three women who could climax through breast manipulation alone. And the other 379 women volunteers didn't mind having their breasts stroked, either. Here is the pattern of breast response in most women:

1. Sex tension first tingles in the nipples.
2. Then the veins around the breast extend.
3. Breasts increase by about one fourth over normal size.
4. The pink or brown area around the nipple enlarges.
5. Whole breast blushes with "sex-flush," a red, measlelike rash.
6. After orgasm, the breasts stay larger for five to ten minutes, then contract to normal.

I said breast size has nothing to do with ability to feel passion! Marilyn Monroe-size breasts may cover a cold heart. Tiny breasts might tingle on the small chest of a tempestuous Audrey Hepburn type. Some men, of course, will always leer after ice-cream-cone mammaries, just as many men will prefer smaller breasts. Does it matter, as long as *your* lover likes *your* breasts? No. The most important factor is that he caresses your bosom the way you like.

*T*here are at least four different caresses for the breast, and each is a different sensation. You or he can conduct an experiment to prove it. Use your wrist (he uses his), and just move the fingers of your hand across the inside of it. That's one sensation. Now, with your tongue, lick your wrist. Then bite gently. Finally, make a kiss. Each is a quite different sensation, isn't it? Now why don't you have a man try these on your breast? (You might repeat the favor for him.)

Every woman has some preference about breast caresses. Here are some *real* women speaking out:

> "So many men pay only perfunctory attention to your breasts before they move on to what they consider more important parts! Really good lovers take plenty of time and know how vital breasts are to sexual stimulation in the female. Bad lovers are terribly irritating when they don't know how to concentrate on this area—you just want to push their hands away and stop them from *plucking* at you! A good lover should be able to distinguish between sighs of pleasure and yelps of pain, but it's amazing how many can't! A man's touch should be feathery and delicate. If you *should* want him to caress you more firmly it's easy enough to indicate your desire by gently pressing your hands on top of his."

> "The bosom for me is a good barometer of how I feel about lovemaking at the moment. If I'm especially receptive, I find

having my breasts caressed and fondled very pleasant; but if I'm not in the mood it can be a very irritating sensation. I think, although I like being petted and caressed, I don't really *crave* that sort of contact. Some women are more responsive to this breast contract—girls who like back rubs, for example—but for women like me a little gentle, loving attention is sufficient to turn me on. Bites and rough handling make me fearful and annoyed."

"There are times when I want my breasts to be handled a little more roughly. Nothing painful or sadistic—just a little abandonment on the part of my lover when I'm totally carried away. I've discovered you have to be *very* careful about asking a man to be "just a little rougher." Some of them take it as carte blanche for a lot of pokes and hard bites and scratches, and if you complain they accuse you of being a masochist! I have no use for this kind of person—he's usually someone who approaches lovemaking with hostile feelings about women and is just looking for an excuse to show his contempt for you. *Please!* When a woman asks you to be just a trifle more aggressive, she means a pale mauve thumbprint, maybe, not scars!"

"Since I nursed my baby my breasts have fallen a little, but I'm going with a lovely man—I'm divorced—who says he enjoys the way they swing and move. He compares them to beautiful pears swinging from a tree. How is that for semantic cool? Sometimes he makes me look in a mirror when he tells me these things, and I feel romantic, sensuous, and flattered. What's more, I know he *means* it! There must be lots of men who would like to reassure their girl friends about their desirability but feel foolish and unsure of how to do it. I guess I'm just lucky."

"I just can't stand men who attack my breasts like a chore to be successfully completed, and then watch me with an eagle eye to see if I'm *enjoying* it enough! It's very important for me to know that the *man* is enjoying it, too. I think that's one of the most important aspects of lovemaking for me— knowing that the man is loving every minute of what's happening between us—that he really *digs* women and me in particular! With a man like that I experience the most glorious, almost orgasmic, sensations in my breasts and nipples.

With the dutiful, detached type of man I feel nothing but an impatience to get it over with. Don't they know the whole thing is reciprocal?"

"The most wonderful lover I ever had convinced me my breasts were fantastic! I have a very average figure and my breasts are on the small side, if anything, but this lovely man raved about them as if I were Sophia Loren! One day he sat down with pencil and paper and drew me the outlines of all kinds of breasts—melons, ice-cream cones, fried eggs—and there were *my* breasts: small, shapely, sweet, and just right. It was a lovely gift from him to me. I still have the drawing and will always cherish it. It was a wise man's way of helping me to overcome those little nagging feelings of inadequacy, and it worked! It made me happy with my bosom and glad to be caressed ever since."

"I like to have my breasts bounced very gently in my lover's hands. I suspect that a girl with large breasts might find this a trifle painful or laughable, but for me there's something so sweet and playful about it—it just turns me on immediately! I don't like painful bites and I *despise* hard pinches on the nipples. I try to guide the man by expressing pleasure (vocally) when he pleases me."

"Lots of men don't seem to realize that it's the *nipple* that's a part of your erogenous zone, not the whole breast. They knead away at the whole area as if it were a loaf of bread. No good! The breast itself can be made to feel delicious and sensual, but the core of all the real sensation is the nipple. For me, the lighter and more delicate a man's touch, the greater the pleasure I experience. Kissing and sucking should not be too vigorous—that vacuum cleaner action some men seem to favor is entirely unnecessary!"

"Because I have such a large bosom, sometimes men tend to ignore the *rest* of me. I hate that. It has made me feel self-conscious and has actually cut down on the amount of pleasure I can feel as a result of breast-play. I want a man to love *all* of me."

All You Can Do for Healthier, Prettier, More Sensuous Breasts
Wise women have *always* known that the breasts had to be given special

care to retain their beauty and softness. (In portraits from the French Renaissance, ladies are shown pinching each others' breasts to see whose are firmest!) Just because they're not *always* showing doesn't mean you can ignore them, does it?

*T*he sixteenth-century beauty Diane de Poitiers, mistress of two kings and at *seventy* described as "still so beautiful a heart of rock would be moved," kept her exquisite body and celebrated breasts so firm and trim she literally *never* aged! Her secrets? We can't all lie in milk and bash our pearls into powder for whitening as Diane did, but we *can* pay attention to the fact that she bathed three times a day in *cold* water, which probably did more to preserve her than anything. Of course, you don't have to go that far, but do remember that bathing the breasts in cold water is an age-old beauty trick that *you* can quite easily do at the end of each bath or shower. (If you're shivering in horror at the very thought, just remember King François I always drank wine from a silver cup modeled after de Poitiers' breasts. It might help!)

A mixture of honey, real cream, almond oil, and rose water was what the lady used to protect her skin. (Breasts saw a lot of exposure then, as now.) *You* can anoint *your* bosom with glycerine and rose water for the same effect. It's bland, mild, silky-smooth, and fragrant—can't possibly harm tender skin. Of course you can experiment; one modern girl *swears* by a product called "Happy Face"—says it's creamy, quick-vanishing, and great for the bosom!

Colognes for the bosom should always be light and elusive fragrances— you may yearn for a musky effect, but men don't want to taste chemically flavored breasts! It's nice to apply fragrance *under* the breasts—it wafts up deliciously. . . . And while you're paying attention to your bosom, make sure you eliminate the little hairs that may grow close to the nipple. You can tweeze them easily, but if the very thought causes you pain, try a depilatory. Warning: *Never* use leg depilatory for your bosom—get the facial variety—or you may break out in rashes that will be as uncomfortable as they are unsightly. (Even with the facial variety, you should test the tenderness of your skin by using a sample amount on a tiny patch of flesh—if there's no reaction, proceed.)

Rashes on the bosom are often caused by slight (and often *temporary*) allergic conditions. Some girls find it impossible to wear *wool* next to the skin without breaking out—usually it helps to wear a shift or camisole-type slip under woolen fabrics in the winter. If rashes persist, you should see your doctor, of course, and not attempt to cover them with cosmetics, which may only irritate the condition.

There are plenty of cosmetics you can use on the bosom. Skillful girls can experiment with regular makeups (blushers, rouges, powders), providing they don't rub off or look *too* obvious. A brush of darker makeup between the breasts exaggerates cleavage—great for small-breasted girls; if you have deep cleavage, use a highlighter on the top slope of the breast —gives a rounder, more *globular* effect—and a cream rouge or a pink glistener (it's transparent) to make the nipples rosy and glowing. If you want your nipples to glow but like them just the color they *are*, try colorless lip gloss for a gilded effect.

Conclusion: Sensuous Thoughts on Your Bosom
- Your lover falls asleep with his head between your breasts.
- You walk up behind him and press your body against his bare back.
- a single rose—in your cleavage
- a kiss—for each nipple
- bare-breasted in a deserted meadow
- a new baby—and a first sweet drink of milk

The Other Erogenous Zones
Actually your entire body is a potential erogenous zone! But some secret nooks and crannies are noted for being *especially* susceptible. These are:
- ears (a love bite on the earlobes? a kiss—with his tongue— deep inside)
- eyelids (sealed with fingertips or a gentle kiss)
- neck (can be nuzzled, or lightly stroked—as you would pet a purring, creamy-throated pussycat)
- waist (meant to be encircled in an embrace)
- hollow in front of pelvic bone (the welcome pressure of his weight here)
- hollow of small of back (a butterfly kiss here, and a wisp-caress or deep massage)
- inside of arm (can be covered with kisses, gentle bites)
- hollow in palm of hand (a cup to receive his kisses, or a sexy palm reading)
- fingertips (to meet his fingertips, or travel fickly over his entire flesh)
- navel (one soft kiss with his tongue)
- thighs (to enclose a lover's flanks, or face, or to receive a tender stroking)

- buttocks (cupped, patted, gently rubbed)
- toes (meant to be tickled, or as Liz Taylor did to Eddie Fisher—sucked)
- bottom of feet (another teasing place to tickle)
- back of knees (touch here, lighter than a butterfly's wings)

Some sex experts say fingertip caresses do most to excite a partner, while palm caresses stimulate the one who strokes and pets. In the nude, the ultimate caress is for your nude bodies to touch ever so lightly at as few points as possible. The more localized the sensation, the more thrill-power. To prove: Rub your hand hard, quickly, several times. Now, take a fingertip and move slowly over the palm. Much more tingly, isn't it?

Sexercises for Mind and Body

Ready for a beautiful orgasm? It's now possible for every woman, thanks to a combination of ancient Oriental rituals with modern scientific sex know-how. If you were a young woman a scant fifty years ago, none of the following sexercises would have been available to you. If you felt *blah* in bed (and most Victorian ladies were supposed to feel worse than *blah*), you were stuck with a bland, or even repugnant, sex life. Thank goodness, you're living *now!* Take advantage of these sexercises for mind and body:

The Uninhibitor. This exercise, a preliminary to *all* fuller release of emotions and sensations, was devised by Manhattan psychiatrist Dr. Alexander Lowen, author of *The Betrayal of the Body.*

Stand erect, with legs about a foot apart, feet turned slightly inward (pigeon-toed). Make hands into fists; put on backs of hips, and (keeping fists on hips) lean back from the waist so that your body arches slightly backwards. Breathe in and out deeply and evenly. Gradually, you will feel as if a knot of tension were slowly untying in your solar plexus. (Your legs may begin to tremble, but don't stop. Hold the position as long as your back and legs can support you without *painful* stress.

Afterwards, to relieve any back strain you may feel, bend forward from the waist, knees slightly bent, toes turned inward a bit. Hang your head down as loosely as possible; reach toward the floor with your fingertips.

Doing this exercise after waking in the morning and before going to bed at night will ease tensions and release some of the blocks against sensation you may have unconsciously built into your body.

The Pleasure Dot. This concentration exercise, which is marvelous for sharpening *all* your mental powers, is best done early in the morning, when your mind is still fresh—*for three minutes only.*

Picture (inside your mind) a small dot of golden-white light, right in the center of your field of vision. Visualize this dot of light as the center of a circle (a ring of golden-white light surrounding the dot). Focus on this circle and the central dot of light. (The exercise can be done with the eyes open, too, but that's hard at first!) Continue as long as you can—maybe only a few seconds at the beginning, but your powers of concentration will improve with practice. When having sex, picture the dot right where the actual pleasure sensation is taking place (usually the genital area). Narrowing your focus to one erogenous area will intensify pleasure.

The Doubled Sensation. Imagine there is an observer inside you; someone who is alert and awake watching what your outer self is doing, aware of everything happening within you and outside of you.

Now—in the course of lovemaking or caresses—let the observer see what you are doing, feel what you are experiencing. The point of this exercise. is *not* a third-person sort of detached observation. The inside observer should *share* your feeling, thus giving a *double* dimension to the pleasure.

Tension Releaser. Lie flat on your back. Close your eyes; relax. Let everything go. Inhale deeply; exhale very slowly. (Compress the muscles of the diaphragm in order to empty every last bit of air from the lungs.) As you exhale, feel your tensions gradually draining from the body, your mind swept clean.

Do ten of these slow, deep inhalations-exhalations. As you lie there, more and more relaxed, visualize your arms and legs becoming very heavy. Think of your mind as a clean, empty sky.

Now—with physical tensions relaxed and the noisy confusion of your mind stilled—try making love. See if sex isn't much simpler and satisfying!

The Mind Expander. Lie flat on the bed with eyes closed, arms and legs relaxed. Breathe in and out very slowly and deeply ten times.

Now focus on your consciousness—on the space within your head. Gradually visualize space expanding so that your being includes the whole room, then your house, street, city, surrounding country; you can do this until your mind has absorbed the entire world, the sky, the universe!

To apply this great meditation exercise to sexual experience, try making love after you have vigorously expanded your consciousness of self . . . you might experience the Cosmic Orgasm!

The Oriental Light. Sit up in bed, with legs crossed in front of you. Close your eyes. Inhale slowly, deeply, and exhale completely—three times. Feel yourself relax, then visualize a clear white light floating and shining about a foot above your head.

1. Now when you breathe in deeply, imagine you are inhaling the light and sending it down to a nerve center at the base of your spine. Exhale, and visualize the light shining out through your body at the end of your spinal column.

2. Inhale again, visualizing the light rising *up* your spine, to a center corresponding to a point in your lower abdomen. Exhale, and feel the light shining out of both this center and the lower one at the base of your spine.

3. Inhale, visualizing the light as moving from your lower abdomen to the bottom of your rib cage, a point corresponding to the solar plexus in front. Exhale, visualizing the light beaming out of *three* centers now (spine base, abdomen, rib cage).

4. Inhale, and raise the light still higher up your spine, to a point near the region of your heart. As you exhale, beam out light and love from this center and from all centers below.

5. Inhale, moving the light up your spine to a point near the region of your throat. Exhale, visualizing the light and love shining out of all five centers.

6. Inhale, raising the light up your spine and concentrating its power on a point in the middle of your forehead between (but above) your eyes. (This is called the *third eye.*) As you exhale, imagine light and love beaming out of this center and all the centers below.

7. Now visualize yourself as moving the light all the way to the top or crown of your head. As you exhale, picture yourself exuding light from these seven centers.

With your next inhalation, imagine yourself lifting up and merging with the light which has been floating above your head.

Do this exercise (which takes *much* less time to do than to describe) *no more than three times,* just before making love. The results are extremely potent when both partners participate in the exercise. After the man has entered the woman, both partners should visualize the light shining out of their seven centers (or *chakras*) and beaming *into* each other's *chakras* while making love. This exercise can generate a truly *total* mind-body orgasm.

Lotus Love. This is the Tibetan yab-yum or Tantric Yoga *maithuna* method of intercourse, in which the man sits with his legs crossed in the Lotus posture. The woman sits down on his lap, allowing his penis to enter her, and she embraces his hips with her legs.

The whole point of this exercise is a prolonged and nearly motionless communion (a true merging and worshiping of each other's total selves) in which the male expends little or no effort. The orgasm that comes after *hours* of slow, easy lovemaking, with a *complete* absence of hurry and force, is truly magnificent. Don't worry about moving; just *feel* the powerful flow and exchange of energy taking place.

*A*ll these meditative exercises and sex positions work *through* your mind to intensify sensation felt by the body. They *block out* your daily, ordinary consciousness of self and create a kind of receptive emptiness, a mental blank page on which pleasure can be exquisitely recorded. After some practice these techniques will lift you out of yourself entirely, so that your mind and body can merge and become one with limitless time and space.

The Magic Muscle Exercise. One sex expert and author says that to continue the buildup of sexual tension, "the woman must surrender to her own drive . . . to seek stimulation emotionally and physically, to seek tension until tension becomes release." *Ah.* But how? *How?*

Use your *pubococcygeus,* a thick (two fingers wide) muscle that surrounds your vagina. Dr. Arnold Kegel, an award-winning Los Angeles obstetrician, accidentally discovered that this muscle, nicknamed the PC, could be exercised to give a woman more sensations in her vagina during sex. The doctor was looking for a cure for poor urinary control. In the process, he taught several women how to contract the PC. They soon reported they could hold their water. Later, the patients whispered to the doctor that there were interesting side effects—sexual ecstasy and orgasm! One woman confided that she had just had her first orgasm in thirty years of marriage! Doctor Kegel wondered why. He studied more women's vaginal muscles and found that in two out of three women he examined, the muscle was weak. To his surprise, the development of this muscle bore no relationship to the rest of the woman's physical fitness. Very athletic, supple girls could have as weak a PC as fat, sedentary women. Frail or flabby ladies could have a powerful PC muscle. The doctor invented a pressure-sensitive tube, called a *perineometer,* to measure the strength of the PC. Most women squeezed out readings from 5 to 15. But the woman with the tight, toned-up PC could push the pressure reading from 30 to 90! If you want to test your vagina-power, go to a gynecologist and get a perineometer reading. You may have weak muscles if you exhibit any of the following symptoms:

- When a man's penis enters and thrusts to and from your vagina, you feel "nothing at all" or "very little."
- You've had several urinary accidents getting to the ladies' room on time.
- Sometimes you wet your pants just by laughing.
- You suspect that a larger penis would make you feel more sensations in your vagina.
- Your sexual pleasure has declined since you gave birth.

Most girls seem to be born with weak PC—other women lose muscle tone when the baby's head passes through the vagina.

*W*hy does the stronger muscle give you more sensations during sex? The answer lies in the deeply buried nerve endings in the vagina. It takes strong pressure to stimulate these nerves. If the muscle is lax, the penis barely makes contact with your vaginal walls. But if the muscle is taut, the penis rubs strongly against the walls and transmits ecstatic messages along your vagina. When you contract the muscle, the stimulation spreads through the surrounding tissues—giving the powerfully sensitive clitoris another boost. Result: super orgasms!

Many primitive societies and exotic cultures know about the "magic muscle" and how to work it. In a few African tribes, girls are not permitted to marry until they demonstrate that their vaginas contract strongly. The Indian *Ananga Ranga* sex manual instructs:

> She must ever strive to close and constrict the Yoni [vagina] until she holds the Lingam [penis] as with a finger—opening and shutting at her pleasure. . . . This can only be learned at great practice and especially by throwing the will into the part affected. . . . Her husband will then value her above all women, nor would he exchange her for the most beautiful queen in three worlds. So lovely and pleasant to the man is she-who-constricts.

"She-who-constricts" is also increasing her own sensations, so everyone is happy! But how do you go about that "great practice"?

*F*irst, see if you can recognize the PC contraction. Since the PC also acts to stop urination, this observation can easily be made in the bathroom. Try to stop your urine flow. If you can (and anyone should be *able* to), you will recognize which muscles are in play. Then learn to contract them under other circumstances. To be sure you're not using the weaker outer muscles to halt your urine, try the maneuver with your knees wide apart. Did it work? Now you're sure that it's the right muscle.

"Once the contraction is learned," says childbirth expert Dr. Mary Jane Hungerford, "it takes little more effort than to close an eye. In fact, it can be done as rapidly as you open and shut an eye, though when exercising, the contraction should be held for about two seconds."

Here's how to exercise the PC:
- Begin by doing five or ten contractions before you get out of bed each morning.
- Also repeat the contractions whenever urinating. "With good control," remarks Dr. Hungerford, "urine can be released a teaspoon at a time."
- As soon as you feel ready, try to have six "sexercise" periods a day—try to do ten contractions each time.
- Step up the program week by week—go to twenty contractions per session until you reach a total of three hundred contractions a day.
- By the time you have been contracting for six weeks, your muscle should be well developed. Even within the first three weeks, many women delightedly report thrills during intercourse.

Once you feel that you have good muscle control, it isn't necessary to continue the deliberate contractions. Your magic muscle will maintain itself once it is strong and healthy. Orgasm will keep the PC contracting happily away.

Now, with your taut new vagina, you should experience more erotic stimulation during intercourse. In addition to adding to your pleasure, these sexercises help prepare you for easy, natural childbirth, if you should ever want easy, natural childbirth. Until then, a happy Yoni and a thrilled Lingam to you and your lover.

How
to
excite
yourself
FIVE

*H*ave you become excited reading this book? We hope so. You've read all about your genitals, and tried lovely touch exercises, so you must be sexually alert by now. And that's one more marvelous aspect of sensuality. The more you *think* sexy, *act* sexy, *look* sexy, the sexier you really will *be!*

Sensuality is its own catalyst. Once you've enveloped yourself in this warm, perfumed aura, you'll keep arousing yourself . . . and the men you want. With a special awareness of yourself as a woman, you'll increase your desire to love and be loved. The rewards for working on your sexuality are self-evident: The more interested you are in your own body, the more you're likely to exercise and improve it. The body looks better, functions better . . . *presto!* It's a sexier body! And the more limber the flesh, the quicker it responds.

It works the same way with your mind. The brain is the number one erogenous zone! By developing sensual *thoughts,* you'll send surefire vibrations. And since sex is a combination of love, affection, friendship, and desire . . . a *little* lust surely helps. On the following pages are listed books, films, music, and other media to help put you in a sexy frame of mind. Some are tender love-ideas, others encourage lustier feelings. See which work for you.

*T*hink of someone or something that excited you in the past: the time Bill made love to you on the dunes . . . or a particular expression in a man's eyes when he looked at you. It can be something as specific as the way one man kissed your breasts . . . or as abstract as that tensing in your stomach when you saw a handsome stranger on the subway.

Many girls easily become excited by movie scenes, passionate novels, or erotic music. Here are some of the most popular media stimuli.

Movie Scenes: Remember . . .

- *On the Waterfront:* when Marlon Brando pressed that girl against the wall.
- *Hud:* when Paul Newman pressed Patricia Neal against the wall.
- *Splendor in the Grass:* when Warren Beatty pressed Natalie Wood against the wall. (It's not the *wall* that's important, but the pressing of body upon body . . . without escape.)
- *Gone with the Wind:* when Clark Gable carried Vivian Leigh up the stairs to bed.
- *From Here to Eternity:* when Burt Lancaster made love to Deborah Kerr in the crashing surf.
- *Women in Love:* when Oliver Reed raped Glenda Jackson after they were *married.*
- *Spartacus:* when Jean Simmons, the slave girl, was offered to Kirk Douglas, the gladiator.
- *Tarzan the Ape Man:* when Johnny Weismuller made love to Maureen O'Sullivan among the bulrushes.
- *Exodus:* when Paul Newman threw Eve-Marie Saint down on that grassy knoll overlooking the Judean hills.

Notice anything unusual about those classic scenes of movie sex? It seems to *me* they're rather male-chauvinist! (After all, they *do* reflect the cultural mainstream!) Now, the man *needn't* initiate sex, and the woman doesn't always have to be pinned underneath him, a receptive vessel for his pleasure or brutality. Maybe you'll be even *more* turned on by *these* movie scenes:

- *To Have and Have Not:* when Lauren Bacall went to Bogey's bedroom and said, "If you want anything, just whistle. You know how to whistle, don't you? Just put your lips together and . . . blow."
- *Zorba the Greek:* when Alan Bates went to Irene Pappas's bedroom at her invitation and learned about lovemaking from the yearning widow.
- *Ship of Fools:* when Simone Signoret went to Oskar Werner's bedroom to take care of him, and they ended up making tender, passionate love.
- *The Lovers:* when Jeanne Moreau took the houseguest into her bedroom, and he made love to her all over her whole body.

- *Blow-Up:* when David Hemmings and two pubescent girls tussled erotically on the floor of his photographer's studio.
- *Five Easy Pieces:* when Jack Nicholson and a silly, lusty girl made love standing up . . . and later, when he and the beautiful musician enjoyed a passionate interlude in *her* room, when *she* was ready.

You probably have some favorites of your own!

Passion-Rousing Books

All-Time Best Sellers (for those who like their sex scenes interspersed with a plot):

- Frank Yerby: *The Saracen Blade* boasts slave girls, harem suits, and lascivious Mongols. *The Golden Hawk* revolves around a girl pirate who was, you guessed it, raped. And *Fairoaks* has a whole plantation full of sultry slaves and lusting owners. Frank's books wax poetic over "hot jets from his loins," . . . "love flesh between her thighs," . . . other throbbing phrases.
- Harold Robbins: especially *The Carpetbaggers.* (Keep your eye on Rina and her giant bosom.)
- Jacqueline Susann: *Valley of the Dolls; The Love Machine.* Jackie consistently comes up with titillating books that tell sordid facts about celebrity high-life.

The Cosmo Five-Foot Shelf of Classics (for those who like their sex scenes interspersed with redeeming literary value):

- D. H. Lawrence: *Lady Chatterley's Lover.* Nobleman's wife has lewd thoughts about gamekeeper, and gets him— royally. Trimmings include flowers on her "mound of Venus," pet names for the genitals involved.
- Henry Miller: *Tropic of Cancer; Tropic of Capricorn; Sexus.* Mostly funky sex in Paris.
- Norman Mailer: a short story called "The Time of Her Time" (included in the volume *Advertisements for Myself*). Mailer-type hero helps a nonorgasmic girl over the hurdle during a couple of sex-marathon evenings.
- Philip Roth: *Portnoy's Complaint.* Funny, yes. Sexy? That too.
- John Updike: *Rabbit, Run,* and its sequel, *Rabbit Redux.* Chronicles of a man named Rabbit and his amours. *Couples:* much marital and extramarital coupling.

Plain Brown Wrapper Books (for those who like their sex unvarnished by niceties of plot or literary greatness):

- *The Story of O,* by P. Reage. Sadomasochism at its height. You'll certainly become more aware of your orifices, as O becomes receptive to all kinds of people and objects.
- *Fanny Hill,* by John Cleland. The ribald classic of Fanny's fanny.
- *Candy,* by Terry Southern and Mason Hoffenberg. A spoof of pornographic books, but still exciting! Follow pubescent Candy's erotic adventures with her guru, gynecologist, and more!
- *The Olympia Reader,* edited by Maurice Girodias. (He's the dear man whose Olympia Press published naughty books in Paris before it was legal to publish them here.) A potpourri—something for every taste!

Unsexist Books for the Sexy Woman:
Perhaps you've noticed that most of these famous books (like many of the famous movie scenes) are products of a *male* point of view. Why *must* rape, he-man brutality, and the Powerful Penis dominate literary sexuality? Why is it always the *man* who initiates the slavish woman into the mysteries of sex? How dare men novelists describe (often falsely) what orgasm feels like to a woman?

We say *phooey!* to male-chauvinist erotic novels . . . but unfortunately they seem to be *almost* the only ones around. Few women have been liberated enough to write openly of their sexual feelings; few men know enough *about* our feelings to describe them. But there are *some* books that don't cater to cultural stereotypes:

- Colette, *Chéri.* An older woman and her lover, a *young* man. She initiates *him* into the pleasures of the senses, from sex to strawberries and cream. A tender, sensuous book for grownups.
- Lawrence Durrell, *The Alexandria Quartet.* Another feast for adult senses . . . *four* books worth! You'll see, hear, smell, taste, touch—all through the flesh-and-blood heroines. Start with *Justine.*
- Violette LeDuc, *Therese and Isabelle.* Boarding-school lesbian eroticism.
- Rosalyn Drexler, *I Am the Beautiful Stranger.* A lusty heroine has *fun* with sex . . . recommended as an antidote to male writers who lecture their female heroines about the profundity and superseriousness of orgasm.

As you can see, the dearth of sexy *unsexist* books indicates real cultural trouble! Hopefully women (and men) writers are hard at work right now to remedy the problem.

There *are* some *other* kinds of books that may help, though:

- *Erotic Art,* Volumes I and II, by Phyllis and Eberhard Kronhausen. These two doctors have collected an astonishing range of art erotica from around the world, *all* cultures, *all* times. Marvelous to curl up with . . . a man at your side. Note particularly the Indian and Japanese prints . . . they're having such fun!
- *The XYZ of Love,* by Inge and Stan Hegeler. An excellent and accurate volume of answers to hundreds of sex questions asked these Danish doctors through their syndicated newspaper column. Some of the responses provide ideas that may turn you and him on . . . read it together.
- Vatsayana's *Kama Sutra.* The ancient (200 B.C.) Indian book on sex practices and customs.

Records to Get You in the Mood

Some girls turn all soft and mushy to jazz, others are stimulated by rock, silky ballads, or the aural caresses of a full symphony orchestra. And of course you probably have your special music that arouses you because it's associated with past sexy circumstances—even country & western or a witty revue lyric can excite you if it triggers the right response! Try these:

- "Begin the Beguine"—an oldie, but the one a cheesecake photographer played to get Marilyn Monroe to pose nude
- The *Abbey Road* album by the Beatles, for lyrical rock (turned up vibration-loud)
- "I Can't Get No Satisfaction," Rolling Stones, for hard, driving rock (but you'll try, you'll try!) Also: the Stones' *Beggars Banquet* album, notably "Stray Cat Blues"
- "Light My Fire," The Doors, or Jimi Hendrix (and they will!)
- Any Billie Holiday record
- Soundtrack, *2001: A Space Odyssey,* which starts with *Thus Spake Zarathustra* by Richard Strauss (good for inner space as well—and what a climax!)
- *Tijuana Brass,* for jaunty matings
- Any Aretha Franklin album
- Janis Joplin, *Pearl*
- *Batucada Fantastica* (Bossa Nova produced in Sao Paolo . . .

ah, those authentic native drums of Brazilian folk culture
. . . wild, wild, wild!)
- Among the classics, try the Liebestod from Wagner's
  Tristan und Isolde; Ravel's *Boléro* (yes, it's a cliché . . . yes,
  it works!) and *Daphnis and Chloe,* Suites No. 1 and 2;
  Schönberg's *Verklärte Nacht;* Stravinsky's *The Firebird;*
  Brahms's Sextet No. 1 in B flat, Op. 18. These are for *le
  moment critique!*

Sensuous Listening Techniques:
- Wear a padded stereo headset—lie in darkness and listen.
- Fall asleep to low-volume throbbings.
- Dance naked to a lively beat.
- Listen together to a car radio—on a rainy night.
- Sip Madeira, fantasize appropriate love scenes as you
  listen.
- Go to an outdoor concert—lie on the grass with him.
- Throw yourself into a hot, tangled mob at a discothèque—
  lose yourself in the rhythm!

The Role of Fantasies
The heroine of Lois Gould's sexy book *Such Good Friends* turned herself on
by reading Krafft-Ebing and working up a sadomasochistic fury. A more
erotically adventurous heroine, played by Catherine Deneuve in Buñuel's
movie *Belle de Jour,* imagined (or *did* she?) that she signed on as an em-
ployee in a French house of prostitution and participated in every form of
sexual activity known to the mind of Western (and Eastern) man! A uni-
versal theme of the submissive female seems to run through most of the
classical fantasies (forcible rape, harem girls, etc.)—but that may well be
the result of total cultural brainwashing! Perhaps deep beneath that layer
of dehumanizing and insipid "socially approved" fantasies you harbor
some truly *liberated* ones you've been afraid to give free play. Let your
imagination run wild . . . and don't repress *any* fantasy just because you
think it's (a) weird, (b) sick, (c) aggressive, (d) funny. You don't *have* to
stay trapped within the sexual-fantasy standards set by *males.* Uncover
your *own* most secret desires . . . fantasy works like an aphrodisiac!

*H*ere are some popular fantasies, with some *new* twists:

• You are a young, supple virgin living in Saudi Arabia. You wear see-
through pink veils and have soft, glowing golden skin. One day, while
walking in your walled garden, you see a handsome young sheik (it

wouldn't do to have a fat old toothless sheik) and give him provocative glances through your veils. He carries you in his arms, lifts you onto a white steed, and rides off toward the palace. There you are shown your satin-cushioned quarters and told to prepare yourself for love. The sheik will return at dusk. You put on more perfume and wait . . . then "let" him do everything, and try some tricks yourself.

• You are an American Indian maiden living in a dark green pine forest. You often bathe nude under a waterfall in a shadowed glen. Seven handsome warriors have been spying on you, thinking you don't see them. (But you *do*, and display your full brown breasts, smooth flanks, round bottom to best advantage.) One morning, the warriors are overcome with desire and drag you into the forest with them. All *think* they're raping you . . . but aha! You're having a good time!

• Now you are a working girl—a French maid. You wear lovely black can-can stockings and bend over a lot when polishing furniture. You bend over once too often, and the young master of the household seizes you and throws you to the soft Oriental carpet which you just vacuumed—and proceeds with oral-genital kisses . . . which is exactly what you wanted him to do!

• During a decadent period (Ancient Roman empire? Napoleonic era?— pick *your* favorite time), you are the most beautiful courtesan in the royal circle. You make love day and night with a series of handsome, well-scented, brilliant men whom you afterward advise on affairs of state. One night, a messenger arrives to say that you are summoned to the King's (Emperor's? Caesar's?) bedchamber. Before you depart, the messenger begs you to caress him first . . . he's adorable!

• In ancient Egypt, you rule as a Princess of the Blood. You go topless and wear only this cute pleated diaphanous skirt. Your nipples are painted red. Your hair hangs thick and black to your shoulders. On your arms, fourteen-karat gold snakes twine sinuously toward your breasts. You often float down the Nile on a barge covered with flowers. One day, you see a handsome youth drowning. You order your servants to fish him out and bring him to you. The rescued boy kneels before you and blesses you. You order him to make love while the oarsmen watch. He obeys, and obeys, and obeys!

• You've really flipped out now—and are living on a distant planet in another stratosphere. The air fills with lavender mist. You are beautiful in a way that no Earth-woman could be—your natural eyelashes are two inches long, your flesh is silken and violet. Hair falls from your head to your heels in long emerald waves. You live alone on your planet, bathing in starlight, until a strange ship lands and handsome black men alight. You teach them to make love in ways that cannot be described here. . . .

• Now you're a young French schoolgirl living at an exclusive girl's dormitory in Avignon. You are a petite blonde with dimples, slim hips, and just-developing breasts. Your roommate, Eve, is a mysterious, golden-skinned brunette with long black braids and an enigmatic smile. She seldom speaks to you. One hot summer night, you are sleeping naked under a sheet. Suddenly Eve is beside you, murmuring, "Ma petite, ma petite." Too startled to protest, you lie still while her gentle hands stroke your nipples. You wish to stop her, but a slow burning inside your body makes the words refuse to come. Her hands float down to your vagina. She murmurs how soft you are, how young. Then her fingers gently tickle and knead you there until you swell and ache so you don't understand what you are feeling . . . then, in a shattering, quivering, diamond-sparkled second, it is all over.

Anything goes in fantasy. It's a healthy outlet for desires you'd *never* act on. So feel free! Fantasize whatever pleases you (lesbianism, group sex, fetishism, voyeurism, exhibitionism)—you'll soon be floating into another hazy realm. A slow warmth will seep through your body. There will be strange flutterings and aches inside. (Of course, some day he'll be so terrific you won't need fantasy at all. Hooray!)

Invent your own fantasies! Here are some useful fantasy elements that turn some people on—but *do* please your own taste.

• Everyone involved is attractive. (No matter how many men you enjoy, there isn't a pimply kid or old geezer in the bunch—unless they turn you on.) And you look *ravishing*. Give yourself long blonde hair, larger breasts, or whatever you think is needed.

• The settings are out of the ordinary. Maybe lush splendor excites you . . . palaces, silky bedchambers, mahogany coaches, marble baths. Or perhaps spartan natural surroundings will work arousing magic . . . a beach by the ocean, the shadow of a forest, snow-covered mountaintop, field of waving daffodils.

• Pick an erotic time period. (Distance unleashes your imagination and impulses.) If your historical knowledge is weak, read about ancient empires . . . study wall paintings from pre-Christian Egypt and Crete. See a few historical movies, or read biographies of Madame Pompadour, Nero, Cleopatra, Marie Antoinette. (Why do you think those historical novels are so popular? *Fantasy-food*—nothing in the plastic present can touch them.) If you *must* be contemporary, fantasize you're among the Beautiful People. Jackie Onassis is a good example of a modern woman living an ancient fantasy. She has the old King *and* the boat, plus sexy harem pants by Valentino and those corny ruby satellite earrings!

When you're suitably aroused by your fantasies, music, books, and movies, it's time to plunge ahead to The Real Thing.

The one giant step toward exciting yourself is masturbation. If you have masturbated, you are deeply in touch with yourself. You know how the currents of desire flow through your body—you react warmly to every light touch of your fingertips. The girl who masturbates enjoys a higher chance of good sex later on—when she has a *man* in bed with her! Until then, you can keep your libido humming with a little self-loving.

In case you have some leftover bugaboos about masturbation, let's clear these up right now. Don't you dare skip this section! If you feel prudish about touching yourself, ask yourself these crucial questions:
- How can you touch a man if you won't touch yourself?
- Do you think you can respond to a *man's* touch if you can't bear your *own?*

If you *still* cling to any doubts or misconceptions, here is the whole story.

"One great thing about masturbation," remarked a character in a recent Broadway comedy, "you don't have to look your best." True. And masturbation offers other bonuses . . . it can provide instant ecstasy when *you* need it, and also help prepare you for less solitary sexual pleasures in the future. This is the ultimate "getting in touch" with your own body.

There's been a sudden healthy public awareness regarding masturbation. Philip Roth's book *Portnoy's Complaint* centered around the tugging of his own organ. And the heroine of Lois Gould's *Such Good Friends* could twiddle herself to fulfillment in "three minutes flat." Now drugstores sport phallic electric vibrators, most likely used for masturbation, *not* muscle massage, and many recent movies depict the solitary pleasure.

As you probably know, masturbation has only recently emerged from under the covers. Not long ago, the act was called "self-abuse," cited as the cause for acne, warts, insanity, and blindness. Young people were warned against the evil dangers of this lonely "sin," urged to use "self-control." Few people talked about *their* masturbation. No one was *talking*—but nearly everyone was masturbating.

Comforting fact: *Almost everyone does it!* Over ninety percent of the men interviewed in the Kinsey report admitted they masturbated; forty-seven percent of the women also confessed. Even though the remaining percentage didn't admit to it, they, too, had masturbated, even if they *believed* they'd *never* touched their own sex organs. The fact: Babies masturbate as soon as their little fingers can reach their sex organs. So even if you can't recall a masturbation experience, it's most likely that you tickled and stroked yourself in early childhood.

You may have repressed the memories of such early masturbation, because mothers in our society often discourage the infant's self-cuddling. It's not true in other cultures—particularly the Oriental and Latin— where cranky babies are actually masturbated by their mothers in order to cease their crying. It works. A touch to the penis or clitoris will bring a beatific smile to any baby's face.

It's tragic that many American parents (yours?) make their children feel guilty about masturbating—which is such a natural, harmless release for sexual tension that it should be prescribed for the sexually uptight. Many doctors recognize this and will treat a celibate woman's "vaginal itch" with strict orders to massage a cream over the affected area. They know it's the massage and not the cream that *cures* the itch, but the patient needs this excuse to touch herself.

If you still can't bear the thought of a sanitary tampon, diaphragm, or vaginal examination, chances are you also have a few bugaboos about masturbation. Let's clear these up right now:

• *Bugaboo: Masturbation is neurotic and immature.*
False. Masturbation is a healthy expression of sexuality. It is appropriate at *any* age. If you are twenty-eight, alone, and frustrated, you're not being "babyish," but practical, to masturbate at night.

• *Bugaboo: Masturbation will spoil you for "real" sex.*
Just the opposite: Masturbation keeps your sexual apparatus in good shape and proves you have no inhibitions about genitals (a good sign). The stimulation helps your body adjust to a nice sexual rhythm. You learn how your body builds to climax, what motions and pressures excite your clitoris and vagina. This practice will help you achieve orgasm better when you're with a man just because your body is *used* to climaxing and

responding. The Kinsey researchers found that only thirteen to eighteen percent of the girls who had masturbated to orgasm during adolescence were unresponsive during marital sex, whereas a much higher percentage of nonmasturbators suffered sexual problems.

Masturbation, when practiced *without guilt,* is such a happy experience that it adds to your general sexual interest. You *feel* sensual in this private knowledge of yourself. You *know* what a hot-blooded creature you are. Later, in intercourse, you will have a real appreciation for how well your body responds because you understand its secrets and its tempo.

• *Bugaboo: Masturbation causes an abnormal orgasm.*
If this is abnormal, right on! Masters and Johnson reported that the *highest intensity orgasms* produced by women in their lab were the results of masturbation (with fingers and penis-substitutes). Because you have absolute control over the stimulation, you can prolong the thrills and heighten the tension as much as you wish.

• *Bugaboo: Masturbation is physically dangerous.*
It would be extremely difficult to masturbate so much that your parts became injured. You naturally fall into a sleepy contentment after climax. Women who wish several climaxes can go on masturbating without any danger. Hazards may involve foreign objects put in the vagina. It's not necessary to use vibrators, phallic objects, anything but your own fingers.

If you've forgotten your early experiences or wish to learn some new techniques, just turn the lights out and experiment. Your masturbation can be as spontaneous as any other sex act. Pick a fantasy, or just picture a sexually attractive man, and proceed to stimulate your clitoral area and whatever *else* you want to touch. It might help you to read a sexy passage from one of the books recommended earlier in this chapter.

Most girls masturbate by gently massaging the area around the clitoris, or the entire *mons veneris.* (The tip of the clitoris is so sensitive that the contact with it is seldom hard or direct.) Pressure may be applied to the shaft of the clitoris, just beside the tip. In addition, some girls insert objects into the vagina, or add sensation by using a feather or a soft piece of silk to stroke the clitoris. And it's not uncommon to masturbate in the bathtub—by letting the tap water run on a throbbing clitoris while you caress yourself.

Nothing is abnormal as far as masturbation goes—if it is *pleasurable* to you. Masturbating is one of the nicest things you can do for yourself.

And, no, it won't make you forget men, or stop wanting one—it's just a logical alternative when a man isn't around.

Your own masturbation naturally leads to a better sex life because it puts you in hot, direct contact with your libido. If you masturbate, you're a girl who loves and understands how her body works. You will be able to perform better sexually with a man, too . . . it's an essential step to ecstasy in bed. And the more you masturbate, the less likely you are to be alone much longer!

*How to
make a man
want you*

SIX

$\mathcal{A}$ll right, you're tingling with sensuality. Now . . . how do you get *him* to tingle back? You don't have to be ravishingly beautiful! *Every* woman is a sexual being, and all you have to do is send out *your* own personal sexual messages, the signals that say, *I am responsive . . . I am warm, loving, giving, I like you.*

If you've followed the suggestions in Chapters One through Five of this book, you do understand and *enjoy* your body. Now you're ready to project this inner eroticism into the cold, gray world. An aura of sensuality will begin to radiate from confidence in your body, an awareness of how healthy and lovely it is, how beautifully it can perform . . . and the man you want will share this awareness. You'll be the girl he turns to stare at. His eyes will lock meaningfully with yours. He'll ask other people, "Who is she?", "How can I meet her?" From the moment he sees you, he will imagine what it would be like to hold and kiss you. He will *want* you.

How do you communicate sensuality, speak its language in every aspect of life? Your body, clothes, apartment, even your office and car, *can* reflect your responsive self . . . conversation, gaze, scent—all emanate the warm message: *I love. I love.* The secret is to project this ardor with subtlety. Men aren't cretins, they don't need—or *like*—to be clouted over the head. The most successful sexuality wafts over a man like a summer breeze. Discreet. Almost mysterious. Think Jeanne Moreau, Anouk Aimée . . . or the fictional Justine. A half-smile, lowered eyelashes—a sudden trapped gaze. Mostly: a secret knowledge that you want the man . . . want to love. *That* conviction exudes from your pores . . . silently; you don't have to hard-sell it.

*T*he beautiful—and intelligent—courtesans of ancient Greece never left the house without preparing their bodies as if to meet a lover. Thus draped in veils and anointed, they usually *did* meet a lover. To do so was *their* principal business. *You* have a much more wonderful existence than *that*—your job and the rest of your wide-ranging modern-girl's life take up so much time that you must be even *more* systematic about being prepared for a man . . . because you *can't* spend half the day in a perfumed boudoir. Make it a second-nature rule *never* to neglect your body; then you won't have to waste precious hours undoing your carelessness.

The knowledge that your body is in wonderfully loving condition will add a secret sexiness to your every move and glance. You *know*. And *he* will *sense* your awareness.

Take this quiz instantly!
- Is your skin soft and lotioned—not dry and flaky?
- Has *all* superfluous hair been removed—even funny stray hairs on your belly, thighs, and around your breasts? (If you know he's excited by body hair—or *you* are—you *may* cater to that pleasure!)
- Are your finger- and toenails clipped and clean?
- Is your hair shiny and sweet-smelling—not sticky with sprays and grime?
- If you're wearing a wig, how is the real hair underneath? (Test: Could you take the wig off and shake your real tresses streaming and free?)
- Are your feet soft—not callused enough to carry you over hot coals?
- Is your underwear a) clean? b) ripless? c) sexy?
- Are your legs unmarred by razor nicks and bruises?
- Can your breath be taken in large doses?
- Is your genital area fresh?
- Have you taken birth control precautions?
- Do you carry a survival kit everywhere? (hairbrush, toothpaste/brush, deodorant, nail file, any makeup you wear)
- Has everything that *you* want deodorized been deodorized?

If you answered "no" to any of these questions, do what must be done. Daily. Automatically, so you don't even have to *think* about it. One smart girl we know wears her diaphragm whenever she goes out—even if she *is* just going to buy groceries. You never know, she says. And "readiness" will save you embarrassment if a man should pop up on a day you thought you were going to see your grandmother.

Too many girls *reject* a man they *want* because he appears unexpectedly and panic sets in: Panties are pinned together! Legs feel stubbly! Horrors! Haven't taken the Pill in three days! *Probably* the dear man wouldn't *mind* the awful truth . . . but it takes a terribly steady ego not to fear he will recoil in disgust. So prepare. Prepare. Even if you haven't even *seen* a man in months. Even if you haven't made love in a year. When you're ever-confident, it won't be long. It could be *today*.

Dressing Your Beautiful Body
You've always known that clothes reflect your personality—but have you considered lately whether yours reflect delight in your *body* and its potential for love? Shouldn't *that* facet of you be expressed in the way you dress?

*T*he clothes you wear can mysteriously affect your state of mind . . . make you feel like a pulled-in, trussed-up nobody or a living, breathing *woman*. Even *accessories* have a psychological affect . . . remember Audrey Hepburn trying to loosen up Humphrey Bogart in *Sabrina:* "In Paris, *never* an umbrella, *never* a briefcase!" For you, that translates into: Never a prim little matronly pocketbook, never *anything* hard or constricting or weighing-you-down. You want to look as though at any moment you are ready to grab a man's hand and rush off with him across the dunes . . . even if the actual confrontation takes place across the Xerox machine! The freer your body feels, the more *alive* you'll be . . . he'll get the right message!

Clothing that excites your senses will excite his, too. You *do* think about visual appeal—colors that are earthy, smoldering (russet, red, cinnamon, plum) . . . blacks and whites to set off the special shade of *you* . . . soft colors that say gentleness (peach, ivory, periwinkle blue) . . . never "acid" anything or muddy hues or hard geometric prints that draw attention to themselves and away from *you*.

But what about the other senses? Feel the caress of fabrics against your skin—cashmere, silk, velvet, velours, chiffon—to remind you, even subconsciously, of your tender body, excite your sense of touch and *his*. Furs and suedes are the natural coverings of sweet little touchable animals . . . and will make a man long to cuddle and caress you. (Try on your fur coat inside out—over a naked body—and remember the sensations when you wear it right-side-up.)

Even sound and fragrance can add to the sensuality of clothing: the languorous pressure of velvet against your legs . . . the elusive scent of raw silk. F. Scott Fitzgerald said he loved Zelda in her sweet-smelling, freshly laundered cotton frocks: Wear a newly ironed and starched piqué sundress over your naked brown skin on a summer evening.

Mostly, remember your body and don't let clothes obscure it from yourself or anyone else. Isadora Duncan, unfettered in her flowing tunics, taught it all . . . her voluptuous figure was not confined in a corset designed to the shape of somebody else's "ideal" body, but freed to experience and respond. Structured underwear and clothing *hide* you from the world . . . *sensual* clothing is only a "second skin."

*H*ave you been dressing *sense*-ibly?
NO if:

- The first time you undress for a man, he is astounded (and delighted) to see the real you . . . at last! "What a beautiful behind!". . ."I thought you were all skin and bone . . . but you're not!" (lovely to hear, but shouldn't he have known?)
- You still love shirtwaists and make them your *uniform*.
- You wouldn't be caught dead without a bra.
- You wouldn't be caught dead without a girdle.
- You and your best friend at the office love to wear identical outfits on the same day.
- You always wear a full slip.
- You tried pantyhose and think they aren't for you.
- Every winter, you switch to flesh-colored wool undies.
- Everything you own is "made to last."
- You buy all your clothes with an eye to "concealing figure faults."

YES if:

- You won't wear anything itchy.
- You can't resist clothes that feel cuddly—long terry robes, cashmere sweaters, soft jersey tops.
- You don't pay attention to size—only the way it fits and looks.
- You could lie down in any dress you own.
- When a man compliments you on your appearance, he says, "I love the way you look," not "What a beautiful dress."
- Friends hug you a lot.

- You feel estranged and alienated in the corset section of department stores.
- Your skirts are several different lengths.
- Your wardrobe isn't divided into one-occasion-only clothes: office clothes, date clothes, beach clothes, etc.
- You could run down the street in most clothes you own—without tripping, teetering, or splitting a seam.

YES, YES (to the point of wretched excess) if:
- You can't walk down the street without being approached by drunk conventioneers wearing paper hats and waving fifty-dollar bills.
- No man has ever brought you home to his mother.
- Hands reach out from manholes and grab at your legs.
- You're sexually molested on the street—*regularly.*
- Cars always honk when they pass you.
- Gas-station attendants peer in at you while they wash the windshield.
- Men make kissing noises at you from doorways.
- Men compliment you on your appearance by saying "Wow, do you look sexy," instead of "You look wonderful."
- You buy most of your clothes by mail from Frederick's of Hollywood.

Yes, there's a line—a wide one—between asserting your body and exploiting it. Flamboyant clothing of the cleave-and-thrust, red-satin-and-black-nylon variety advertises you as available to one and all . . . which you aren't. Isn't the whole *idea* to attract the man who will want *you*, not the undiscriminating fellow who will lurch toward the nearest available wares on display? General rule: The more there is of you, the more discreet you must be. A ninety-pound weakling can carry off that slinky slashed-to-the-waist, slit-to-the-thigh, white crepe Jean Harlow dress. A Rubens blonde in the same dress would look like a hooker. (Manufacturers shouldn't even *make* those clinging numbers in size sixteen, but they know some of us will wedge into anything!) It's a question of sexual symbols: Fair or not, overripe nectarine breasts and bouncing-melon derrières are potent sex symbols to *start* with. A supersex dress compounds the symbolism to the point of erotic overkill—and you end up being a *caricature* of sex. (Germaine Greer calls that a female female-impersonator.) You lucky *voluptuées* would look sexy in a giant green plastic Baggie . . . while the girls fighting the *mistaken* assumption that skinny-isn't-sexy really *need* the cling, the cleavage, the see-through.

Renoir bathing-beauty or Modigliani enchantress, you're wearing anything too tight if a panty line shows through . . . smooth lines always . . . unless the effect is perfectly calculated. Jacqueline Onassis is said to prefer a hint of bikini-panty outline under her meticulously tailored Jax pants, and if you're an elegant type, you might be able to bring off the same delicate suggestion.

Contrast and contradiction are tension-creating, hence interesting and sexy. Under a transparent look-at-me pink blouse, a pink-and-white gingham bra says "Which am I? Temptress, little girl . . . or both?" (A black lace push-up number under the same blouse would simply convey the message, "Look . . . I'm desperate enough to let you see my underwear!") With hotpants that bare your long limbs, a turtleneck sweater is elegant, where a see-through blouse would simply create a relentlessly *naked* effect. Mix demure with daring. Wear only *one* "sexy" thing at once.

You'll also want to exercise a little discretion about *where* you go in *what.* The tank top that outlines your nipples may be fine at a sleek beach party (remember the picture of Jackie in Portofino?) but will net cold stares at the office staff meeting. The *only* place for see-through that actually can be *seen through* is at home for a private tryst.

*A*ll your clothes should *move* well . . . flow and fall, or cling to your body and move as part of *it.* Nothing should bag, wrinkle, or pucker. Above all—clothes should make *you* feel desirable and comfortable. Here are some additional ideas:

- cashmere sweater over naked breasts
- see-through underwear—under a schoolgirl jumper
- opaque dress—with see-through sleeves
- golden suntan, backless dress
- scarf instead of blouse, tied in a halter at neck and waist
- full skirts—under a bare midriff and skimpy halter
- wide-cut armholes that display a pretty flash of breast at each side
- crocheted bikini playing hide-and-seek with your secrets
- wet T-shirt plastered to tanned body
- voluminous caftan—and naked you underneath
- strategic pockets on a sheer blouse

*I*t's not just what you put on your body, but the condition it's in as well. "Health is very sexually attractive," says one of the best experts I know, a man who is absolutely crazy about women. (Isn't that all the credentials he *needs?*) Your posture and walk should convey: *My body is in prime condition. It feels good. I am proud of it.*

When sex was only for "bad girls," a sullen tubercular slump struck the correct note of depravity and dissipation needed to allure. But now that we know sex is healthy and normal, the sexiest girl is energetic, vital. So chin up! Shoulders back! Rib cage out! Breasts high! Tummy in! Hips tucked under! Don't shuffle along as though you were in the last stages of terminal depression, or slither along like a twenties vamp doped to the gills on opium. Look alive! (Think Julie Christie in the film *Billy Liar,* swinging along a street, free and flowing.)

Besides, doctors say that sexless posture actually deforms your body. Stoop today, droop tomorrow. Slumping causes dowager's hump and saggy breasts. Good posture is more firming than a forty-dollar girdle. And a word from the psychiatrists: Posture that is closed inward (lowered head, concave chest, downturned shoulders) shuts out the world, says "Don't bother me, I'm too engrossed in my own problems." So use the language of your body movements to convey interest in people and they will respond. Here are some lessons in movement:

• Observe any house cat. Watch this silky little creature roll languorously on her side, stretch her long lovely body, sit up daintily . . . and walk about with the air of being queen of all she surveys. A cat knows instinctively how to move sensuously. When resting, she sinks into a suitably flattering pose. See how she flings her head back to expose a soft creamy throat, walks—quickly—but with the fluid grace of slow motion. She's relaxed yet alert, loose and taut at the same time . . . makes all who see her want to hold and stroke her.

• Sexually attractive movement doesn't have to mean sexually *provocative* movement—rotating your torso or wiggling your rear like a kitty in *heat!* Observe *men* in motion and discover what you love about the way they move *their* bodies. Watch Rudolph Nureyev or Edward Villella dancing . . . Arthur Ashe stretching for a tennis serve . . . Bobby Fischer handling a chess piece with gentle, constantly moving hands . . . basketball great Bill Russell, even *off* the court on a TV talk show, fluidly crossing his legs, throwing back his head to laugh . . . a long-legged stranger dodging traffic . . . your lover's motions as he crosses a room, pushes back his hair, runs to meet you. If a *man* doesn't have to grind his pelvis to arouse you, what makes you think your movements can't be exciting in subtle ways, too? Fantasize: Imagine you are . . .

- weightless—floating on a cloud.
- barefoot on new spring grass.
- lying on eiderdown.
- underwater.
- being carried by a strong man into a crashing ocean.
- floating on a raft.
- walking over violets.
- basking under summer sunshine.
- riding a barge down the Nile.
- rolling down a snowdrift.
- free-falling from an airplane.
- sleeping on satin sheets.

Walk light. Lie soft. You have no angles—only curves. Curl up. Stretch out. When you are reclining, you are waiting to receive your lover. When in motion, you are moving toward him . . . very nice!

Your Apartment: A Place for Love
Yes, your apartment is *yours* . . . a private retreat, a haven from the world's hassles. But you don't want it to *exclude* others—especially not that wonderful man. Just as you keep your body ready for your lover, keep the apartment ready to welcome him into your life, a place where he will want to love you.

Look sharp, take drastic steps if any of the following are in view:
- your wig collection—mounted on styrofoam heads
- stuffed animal collection
- cat's litter box
- dog's rubber toys
- your high-school graduation photo
- your sister's wedding picture
- exercycle
- three-year-old collection of *TV Guides*
- that rubber sweat suit that was supposed to shrink your hips
- portable clothes dryer—draped with pantyhose and undies
- electric beauty equipment: hair dryer, facial sauna, sun lamp, electric rollers, shaver
- enough potions to stock a beauty-supply house
- dress dummy and yards of material
- open ironing board, pile of laundry

Naturally you may *have* some of these things (what are you doing with *all* of them?!)—but hide them! Men panic at the sight of beauty-maintenance paraphernalia, pet junk, sentimental keepsakes. Of course, an individual man may love playing with your cat or think it's hypocritical to hide your laundry—if you *know* him that well, fine. Otherwise, considerately spare him the sight of junk he *may* think is silly. *Some* don'ts apply to *every* man:

Things You Must Not Have Around. Period.
- your mother or other relatives
- female roommates
- a single bed
- a cradle
- pink ruffles
- dolls
- a hospital bed
- wax fruit
- plastic flowers
- antimacassars
- plastic slipcovers

Man-Pleasers
Men will snuggle in happily if your apartment puts them at ease. Try:
- comfortable chair (Men fall over themselves to slide into a recliner or a chair with an ottoman.)
- king-size bed, or extra-long queen-size (for big men, active loving)
- long, cushy sofa (for extended cuddlings)
- well-stocked bar (dry vermouth, gin, Scotch, bourbon, his favorite imported beer, soft drinks if he's a nondrinker)
- stereo—and headsets for sense-pleasing listening
- men's magazines (to keep him busy while you're cooking or dressing)
- shaggy rugs, huge floor pillows—for lazy afternoons
- working fireplace, logs and kindling handy

Avoid like the Black Death: pink, chintz, "busy" florals. These designs may be beautiful, but they make men "itchy." Colors men love: bone-beige, ivory, russet, gray, smoky blues, earth, red. Textures they crave: leather, suede, velvet, fur. Men seem to react more to the way a room *feels* than the way it looks. Stress comfort and coziness over chic design. Throw out china knickknacks and donkey plant-holders.

Romance-Inspirers

A romantic look needn't depend on pink damask and plaster nymphs. Try these decorating hints:

- soft, flattering lighting (Indirect light works best, but low-level lamps with dim, rosy bulbs will also create a warm mood. Candles give a romantic glow, too.)
- lush, green jungle plants (Greenery creates a Garden-of-Eden climate—passionate!)
- good, soft bed linens (Solid shades, tiger stripes, art nouveau, designer prints—all work. Satin sheets feel good and are fun—as long as the rest of your bedroom isn't done in Early Bordello. Men usually don't like teensy florals or circus-clown designs, although the latter are considered amusing high chic by one terribly jaded man I know.)
- tall candles—to be lighted in the dark of night
- a mirror—on a rolling stand to swing over to the bed for erotic glimpses
- an exotic, authentic print of a classic Oriental or Indian passion scene (But *do* be careful not to create an over-bearing pleasure-palace effect with too much erotica on display!)
- stereo controls within reach of bed
- a breakfast tray for lazy mornings
- titillating extras: water pillow? Swedish featherbedding? an ornate brass headboard? subtle strobes? a lava lamp?
- heavy window coverings—to screen out light and shut in privacy; romantic shutters, flowing draperies; anything but those *dumb* Venetian blinds!

The "loving room" should be a world unto itself. A quiet, cushioned place where lovers have an endless night to explore one another . . . .

The rest of your apartment should be man-proofed. This is just a matter of tact: (1) You want him to be comfortable; (2) you *don't* want him to be embarrassed by the sight of superpersonal items when he doesn't yet feel really intimate with you.

The Bathroom

Keep a special cabinet (not the main medicine chest): an antique wood box, or a wicker one, or some other hideaway (the linen closet, perhaps) for personal gadgetry. Feminine hygiene should be discreet—put away all tampon boxes, vaginal deodorants, birth-control pills. Also nervous-making to a new man: "serious"-looking prescriptions, ointments, blemish creams, wart removers, depilatories. Many a man has reeled back at the sight of—hemorrhoid cream, blackhead remover, athlete's-foot-fungus powder, asthma respirator, tranquilizers, sleeping pills, false-tooth cleaner, diet pills, hypodermic syringes. *Do* have on view: vitamin tablets, herbal mask, massage cream, organic freshener . . . anything that reflects vibrant *health*. When the man stares into your medicine chest, he should see only a bright, sunny reflection of yourself. You may indeed be a greenish, allergic, wheezing thing, but there's no need for *him* to know. (Maybe *he'll* be so therapeutic you'll be able to throw *away* those disorder-remedies *forever!*)

Stress cleanliness in the bathroom. Your dusty living room may elude a man's notice, but he'll feel trapped by a ring around the bathtub. Keep porcelain shining. Include these refreshing, thoughtful bath accessories:
- giant, thick bath sheets—the kind that are big enough to wrap around a big man
- cakes of unscented soap . . . or masculine scents, like sandalwood and pine
- big, fluffy bath mat, for his big feet
- extra toothbrushes, still in cellophane
- shaving soap and lather brush, in antique wood dish
- extra razors, clean razor holder
- personal drinking glass
- mini-bottles of vodka, crème de menthe, for intoxicating gargle
- hose attachment in shower, or spray nozzle over shower faucet, for "needle-sharp" rinses
- long-handled bath brush or rough, natural "loofah"
- terry kimono—one size fits all!
- bathroom scale—adjusted to read five pounds lighter than actual weight

Guaranteed—your man will come bounding from the bathroom, fresh and virile! One fiendishly clever girl keeps her bathroom dimly lit and knowingly hangs a shaving mirror that *narrows* any reflection. All men emerge looking lean and rugged—or at least *thinking* so.

Keep after your bathroom. It's boring work, but certainly beats cringing in the living room while a man flounders among cosmetics, dripping underwear, and soggy bath mat. Doesn't it?

The Kitchen

Yes, that functional room the kitchen *can* have an aphrodisiac effect on a man. Even if you don't spend every spare hour whipping up tantalizing soufflés, you *can* have a kitchen a man will like to be in, stocked with plenty of things he'll love to eat. (Don't try to fool him with expensive equipment if you can't progress beyond canned soup and diet malts . . . it isn't worth the money, because he'll only feel duped when he discovers you *can't* make him a flawless omelet at one A.M. If you find out *he* likes to be chef, by all means provide some sturdy standard equipment.) Of course, if you *are* an apprentice Julia Child, *flaunt* it. Visions of gourmet meals never scared any man away—especially if you actually produce one now and again.

If you *do* cook well and often, you probably already have (or are steadily acquiring at whatever pace your budget can stand) lots of marvelous pots, pans, a cheese grater, pâté molds, and other attractive kitchen delights. *Display* them! But if you hardly *ever* cook, the kitchen still needn't look like a one-room ghost town. That doesn't mean "decorating" your refrigerator with a velveteen throw! Men, lucky creatures, have not been raised (like many *girls*) to think functional objects have to be concealed with frills and flounces to be beautiful; they *like* useful things for their own sakes. Try culinary-object decor to *really* please a man. (Even an I-never-cook girl will find these things useful):

- wire whisks hanging on wall (Even a so-so cook can use these for beating eggs.)
- miniature herb garden on windowsill (Smells and looks delicious even if an herb never passes your lips.)
- cookbooks, including classics—Julia Child's *Mastering the Art of French Cooking,* Michael Field's *Cooking School, Larousse Gastronomique* (Buy paperbacks if you don't want to invest too much money. Fannie Farmer's *Boston Cookery School Cookbook* never did anybody any harm. The whole matter of cookbooks is like having a few magazines that *you* don't read but *others* do—who knows when a *man* may want to serve *you* eggs Benedict in bed?)
- spice rack—glass bottles filled with stick cinnamon, whole nutmeg, black pepper kernels, basil, bay leaves, and more!
- wire salad-drying basket

Men feel faint when they open a refrigerator and see your pitiful little grapefruit-half and two pints of yogurt. Keep some of the following non-perishables around for men. (If you're dieting, select from the list those foods you hate, *really* hate.)

- hearty canned soups (Minestrone in large quantities has never failed me! Neither has a good black bean soup, spiked with good sherry.)
- frozen shrimp, crabs, oysters
- frozen Mexican food (tacos, enchiladas, etc.)
- cans or jars of marinated artichoke hearts
- pickled mushrooms
- canned corned-beef hash (delicious with eggs for breakfast)
- canned chili
- grits (for Southerners)
- spaghetti or linguini
- spaghetti sauce in cans or jars (can be doctored with Italian sausage, onions, ground meat, green pepper, mushrooms, and those herbs you thought you'd never use)
- canned ravioli (not bad, not bad at all)
- baked beans (make a man feel homey and secure)
- hamburger (frozen in waxed-paper-wrapped individual-portions to thaw in a hurry . . . not to be tried without a separate freezer compartment; the temperature in a little ice-cube-tray compartment isn't low enough for long-term freezing)
- canned pâté (chilled in the icebox, served with pepper and a light grating of nutmeg)
- canned mussels
- a small hard salami, Danish or Italian (keeps in icebox up to six months)
- canned deviled ham

Things that bode ill in the kitchen
- rat- or mousetrap on floor
- odor of roach spray
- slop-over drips on stove, counters
- industrial-type garbage can
- TV-dinner wrappers
- filthy cupboards

The Car That Drives Men Wild

One man I know tells me he thinks it's terribly sexy for a woman to drive. (He didn't even say "drive *well*"!) When I asked him why, he said, "There's something about the *autonomy* of a woman driving—especially if it's her own car . . . I get the feeling she's her own woman. I guess independence is sexy." Right on!

If you *don't* have a car, but are planning to buy one, you're acquiring a possession that will naturally make you attractive to men. When buying, consider the *image* of your car:

- Sports cars are sexier than sedans.
- Foreign cars are sexier than American cars.

If you want the breakdown by nationality, car sex appeal goes as follows:

- English: elegantly sensuous
- Italian: peppy, red-hot
- French: erotic—a challenge to control
- Swedish: husky, rugged, ready for anything
- German: practical, very smooth
- Japanese: cute, eager

But if you can only *afford* that 1952 Chevie, take heart: *Any* mobility is sexier than *none!*

If you already *have* a car, give it a long, hard look. Is it really *you?* Does it cry out, "Take me on a lazy weekend!"? "Drive me to the beach at midnight!"? "Elope with me!"? My friend Ruth finally had to give *up* her $250 used-car bargain (purchased in desperation when she needed immediate transportation to and from a wonderful but distant new job): "Every time I got behind the wheel," she said, "I felt like I'd aged twenty years, gained forty pounds, and my hair had turned blue. There was *no way* you could look chic in that car!"

Take severe measures if *your* car has:

- shark fins
- two pastel colors
- more than ten feet of chrome stripping
- oxidized paint
- "I Like Ike" stickers
- dangling religious statuettes, stuffed animals, other car "novelties"

You remove the gimmicks. A visit to the nearest body shop or garage can remedy the other eyesores.

Additions to your car can enhance its sex appeal:

- real leather upholstery
- comfy seats
- AM-FM radio
- stereo tape deck
- well-tuned, murmuring engine
- fluffy lap robes

Be sure your pretty little car is *running*. There is nothing appealing about a car dragged by a tow truck, or limping along the road. A breakdown on the freeway at eleven P.M. on a Sunday evening can spoil the mood of the most romantic weekend. Make tune-ups as much a part of your life as dental checkups.

Keep your sexy little car shiny-clean. Use leather conditioner on the upholstery. A lemon polish smells divine. Keep after ashtray accumulation and car flotsam—road maps, soda cups, crumpled tissues, sandy floor.

Drive in a businesslike way—the road is no place for "cute" "female" incompetence (unattractive at the best of times, downright dangerous at the wheel). Men admire a girl who's no-nonsense about cars: The contrast to the soft, pretty way you *look* is superappealing:

- Keep a sure grip on the wheel, a keen eye on the road.
- No girlish shrieks: "Ooooh! A Mack truck!" "Ooops, we passed Pick-a-Pair of Shoes!"
- If you need glasses, *do* wear them for driving. The penalty for vanity is too high. (If you *hate* yourself in glasses, get contacts.)

Secure in your skill, you can afford a few frills that will make you as seductive as those women who were always passing James Bond in fast Ferraris:

- leather or string openwork racing gloves
- shorts or miniskirts to reveal your legs—seductively long as they work the accelerator and brake pedal
- a scarf flying from your throat—but not long enough to strangle you by catching on the wheels Isadora Duncan–style or obscure your vision
- big, beautiful sunglasses (for daytime driving only . . . they're trouble at night)
- a little wrapped turban to keep your hair from frizzing

Aphrodite Among the File Cabinets, or: How to Be Alluring in the Office Without Actually Hanging Black Satin Sheets on the Wall
You meet men at your office. New men. Or old buddies who surprise you with that "Why, it's been George all along" feeling. How do you make your office—and your office manner—say "I am an individual, wonderful, sense-loving woman"?

Make the office as appealing as possible. Kill that battleship gray that surrounds you like armor. Splash! Splash! Color everything you can wave a paintbrush over! Bring in—plants! pictures! posters! rugs! goldfish!

Mirror, mirror, on the wall—needed in the office most of all. When you're slaving away, you often muss your hair (or tilt your wig) or smear ink on your face. Result: You emerge looking like Lizzie Borden and never know it. Keep a mirror within winking distance of your desk. Check. If you have a door, indulge in a long, full-length mirror. That way you won't stagger out with drooping pantyhose, dangling slips, or worse. An unwitting secretary we know once walked out of her office dragging a roll of adhesive tape from her derrière.

Keep the office as sensuous as possible without losing efficiency. Skip fur pillows, scented candles, stereo headsets. (A whole magazine *folded* once because everyone tuned in at work.) And sorry—keep the fluorescent lights glaring. You do have to *see!*

Naturally you must tailor these suggestions to your specific office. In some hierarchies, the rug, sofa, lamp, are status symbols reserved for top executives . . . and you'll look pushy if you import such decorations into your little administrative-assistant's cubicle. Use judgment and tact. *Many* companies will thwart nearly *every* effort, demanding that *all* employees inhabit identical whitewashed cells unadorned by signs of life or personality. I once worked for a company housed in a super-high-rise, where one fellow-drudge was reprimanded for having a cartoon taped to his *telephone;* we had to clear our desks at night, and *nothing* could be hung on the walls—seems the cleaning force was temperamental. If you're working in such a place, here are some little suggestions for circumventing the rules without losing your job. (All objects can be tucked away in a drawer at night):

- Make visitors feel welcome with nonperishable tiny snacks on hand for special company: wrapped mints or hard candies . . . nothing that will melt, rot, attract roaches, or is so luscious you'll eat it all by yourself. (Choose a goodie you're not fond of—something you're *allergic* to is better; most office girls will gobble *anything* at 4:35 p.m.!)
- Who could object to a desk clock? Make it a pretty ornamental one with a lovely Roman-numeraled face.
- Use ashtrays of crystal, or Limoges saucers. (Odd ones can be picked up for pennies at antique stores.)
- Fill a little wicker basket or silver porringer with paper clips and rubber bands.

- Use a pretty paperweight (a flower encased in Lucite, a chunk of quartz, or a *mille fleur* paperweight).
- Change that desk blotter. Try daffodil yellow or Tahitian coral instead of hospital green.
- Keep a pretty appointment calendar, like the ones put out at Christmas by the Museum of Modern Art and Metropolitan Museum. (No, you *don't* have to use that standard plastic ring-binder number that came with the desk!)
- Spray the office (discreetly) with your perfume.

No, your office is *not* your home. No boudoir effects, please! Acres of pink silk will make male fellow-workers feel *uncomfortable* rather than sexy. Avoid:

- ruffled lampshades
- photos of dear lovers and parents (unless you're working for them)
- illuminated makeup mirrors or magnifying mirrors
- a vanity-table skirt around your desk
- collections of any sort, unless it's something as simple as a few exotic shells collected on your vacation—remove after a few months, anyway!
- personal desk clutter (cosmetics, hand lotion, fingernail polish, souvenirs, love letters)
- movie- and pop-star pinups—they're for teenagers!

Short of these disastrous errors, you'll have to draw your own line between a pleasant-to-be-in office and a mindless froufrou one. Men *do* like to see personal touches . . . and talk to you about them. ("What a hardy plant to survive so well in this airless building!" . . . "Where did you get that wonderful little primitive painting!")

In fact, such additions to the office environment are simply *civilized,* and it's too bad more *men* don't indulge in them, too. (Perhaps many men have been so overwhelmed by the dog-eat-dog business philosophy that they've *forgotten* about the *amenities* that make daily routine a little less *boring!*) You *will* notice that top executives who have personality and character do have "decorated" offices—oriental rug, a hammered-brass coffee table, a painting or two . . . the more *time* one spends in an office, the more pleasant the surroundings must be. So don't fear that your art nouveau poster will convince the boss you're neglecting office duties! The five minutes spent hanging the poster will probably prevent *hours* of future shock from gazing at a mass-produced module wall.

Talking Manners

Wherever you meet the man you feel a *pull* toward—at work, on the beach, at parties—you must be able to do more than simply *talk* to him. If you want to know him better, you must convey this desire, create a glass bell of intimacy that shelters the two of you together, apart from all the others.

Always try for dulcet tones. Remember: Whispers speak louder than shouts. Whisper *anything* and it sounds erotic. One fabulously successful seductress always sidles up to her man at parties and whispers something perfectly mundane ("Wonderful party, isn't it?"), sinking the words velvetly right into his ear. The whisper is Instant Intimacy . . . a soft promise that the two of you will soon be close—in love, in bed . . . . (*Do* be careful not to whisper *all* the time, though—you'll devalue its impact and he'll think you're dotty!)

Other intimate maneuvers:
- When he's speaking, watch his *lips* instead of his eyes.
- While you speak to him of business, sports, or books, imagine how he would make love to you.
- Fix his tie—without mentioning it.
- Touch his cheek lightly. (He'll kiss your fingertips.)
- Offer an hors d'oeuvre—straight to his lips.
- Touch your own lips with your fingertip before you speak. (He'll think of kissing you.)
- Move in close enough to smell him.
- Hold his wrist so that you can see what time his watch reads.
- Look down at his feet, then suddenly right into his eyes.
- Let your hair down while he's watching you.
- Ask him to hold something for you—something sweet and fragile, something of yourself—your chiffon scarf, a crystal goblet, a tiny filigree purse.
- Stop in the middle of a sentence and let the sexual tension grow between you.

Now, he *will* want you . . . so read on!

*Know
his body
nude*

SEVEN

$\mathcal{N}$ow you understand your own sexy body, know how *you* feel during lovemaking, and what you like. Caresses. Orgasms. You understand every shiver and tingle. But what do you know about your lover?

If you're like most girls, very little. You were trained not to look at "the thing" during childhood. And you've been conditioned not to ask about "it" ever since. You may have experienced only the most covert glimpses of naked men—in the dark, in the shadows of a park, under covers. Many women *still* avert their eyes. Others stare but don't really understand a man's genitals. They *see* him, but he might as well be a Martian (with that strange apparatus dangling between his legs!)—for all they actually know about his sexuality.

Just as your body can respond to erotic caresses, your man's body is equally sensitive. Too many misguided girls think that only *females* deserve light cuddling, kissing, and holding. They don't realize that a man (even a big, burly one) still needs and deserves tenderness and a sweet, special effort to arouse him as lusciously as possible.

All your erogenous areas (nipples, inside of ear, etc.) are also erogenous for him. Don't let him do all the petting. You'll add to your own pleasure and his if you explore his flesh and excite him. Just think how marvelous his body is . . . how different in its own exciting way from your own precious self.

Do you know how he's different from you? How orgasm feels to a man? What happens to his body when he makes love? Which sex organs are most sensitive? You're dying to know, so here, at last, is a simple explanation of what happens to *him* when he makes love.

But before we plunge into the mysteries, here's a rundown on:

Things You Probably Know (But Better Be Sure Of . . .)
In case you've been sequestered in an all-girl retreat and have never seen a naked man, this is what he has that you don't: a penis, a scrotum, and testicles. He's also put together a bit differently—his urethra runs down his penis, and is used both for urinating and ejaculating semen. (A man can't urinate while he has an erection, though.)

The penis is a man's main sex organ. The tubelike length is called the shaft; the acorn-like tip is the glans head. The urethra is inside and runs along the underside, ending in the tiny opening at the penis tip. In an uncircumcised male, a foreskin covers the head of the penis; it's pushed back for cleaning the head. In a circumcised male, the head is exposed. The penis shaft is covered with soft, pliable skin, while the head is covered by a special type of skin called erogenous tissue—found also on the female clitoris and on nipples—with special nerve endings that cause it to respond erotically when stimulated. Where the head meets the shaft of the penis, it widens to form a ridge, called the corona.

Now for the most sensitive part of the whole penis-structure: On the underside of the penis, you'll see that where the head is joined to the shaft, there's a cleft or groove. At this point a membrane called the frenum connects the head to the skin of the shaft. (On an uncircumcised man, the frenum connects the head to the foreskin, and can be seen by pulling the foreskin away from the head.) The frenum is linked to a mass of nerves that make this a supererogenous part. Stroking the frenum or flicking it back and forth will arouse a man very rapidly.

Another area you should know about is called the perineum—that's the ridge between the base of the scrotum and the anus. (You have one, too—between your vagina and anus, but yours is much less sensitive. We'll tell you why.) In some men, stroking of the perineum can cause immediate erection and even orgasm. In fact, any man's body is especially responsive in the whole rear area: base of the spine, anus, buttocks, and of course perineum. That's because so many erection-causing nerves are located here, and because the rectum passes quite near the prostate gland, which reacts (pleasurably so!) to pressure. (Many men enjoy having their orgasm intensified by a lover's finger pressing on or probing right into the rectum. That's one reason why male homosexual activity is more pleasurable than it might seem to the uninitiated observer. *You* can use that information to please your *heterosexual* man if you—and he—would like it. It's perfectly normal and fine!)

$\mathcal{A}$s far as arousing your man by touching his genitals, we will tell you much more about that in Chapter Nine. For now, just remember that with most men, direct penile caresses should be kept light and gentle at the beginning—the penis and especially the tip are so exquisitely touchy that you may speed his climax too swiftly. If you *know* your lover has little difficulty maintaining his erection without reaching orgasm, you can devote more attention to a firmer stroke and gentle pulling along the penile shaft, cupping caress of the tip, circling strokes around the corona, massaging motion around the entire organ, up-and-down movement of the penis skin on the shaft. You can even run your finger along that little cleft . . . and don't forget the fabulous frenum! What else can you think of? Aren't men marvelous? Aren't you glad you're loving one?

You will notice, when caressing the penis, that clear, colorless drops of liquid often emerge from the tip shortly after erection. This is not semen, but a secretion from the glands lining the urethra, and its purpose is to lubricate the passageway of the sperm so that when orgasm does take place, the semen can be ejaculated easily.

The sperm is produced by two egg-shaped glands called testicles. They are about two inches long, one inch wide, and less than one inch thick; and they hang in the fleshy sack called the scrotum. The skin there is wrinkled and may be fuzzy with hair. (When a man is aroused, the scrotum contracts and the skin appears more taut. The same thing happens when he's cold, even if not sexually excited.) The scrotum varies greatly in size. Some men have very large ones that swing between their legs; others have high, tight bags. Most men enjoy a scrotal stroking very much, provided it's gentle. *Don't* squeeze—unless he asks you to!

You probably *knew* all that, but it never hurts to be sure. And it *can* hurt to have misconceptions about the opposite sex. Many girls have really kooky ideas about men's genitals. These false ideas are just as common as they are wrong. Straighten yourself out with the facts. Get rid of:

Phallic Fallacies: Things You May Have Believed That Just Aren't True
• *Big men have big penises.* False: The size of the penis has no relation to the man's height or weight. Some huge men have tiny penises—and vice versa.
• *Big penises are more exciting than little ones.* Only in the eyes of the beholder. The small ones enlarge more than the big ones, so in the end they measure out about the same.
• *Circumcised men can't control their ejaculations.* Not true: They're absolutely splendid.
page 109

External Male Genitals

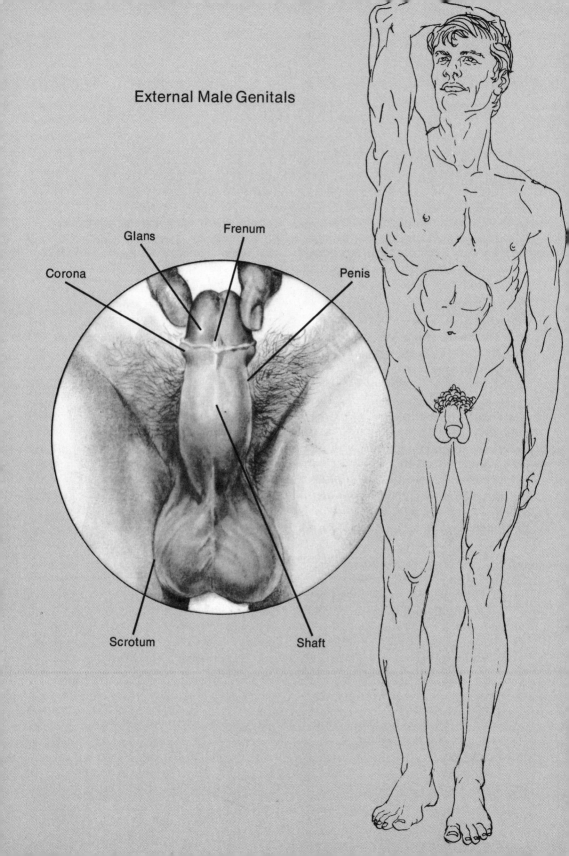

Glans

Frenum

Corona

Penis

Scrotum

Shaft

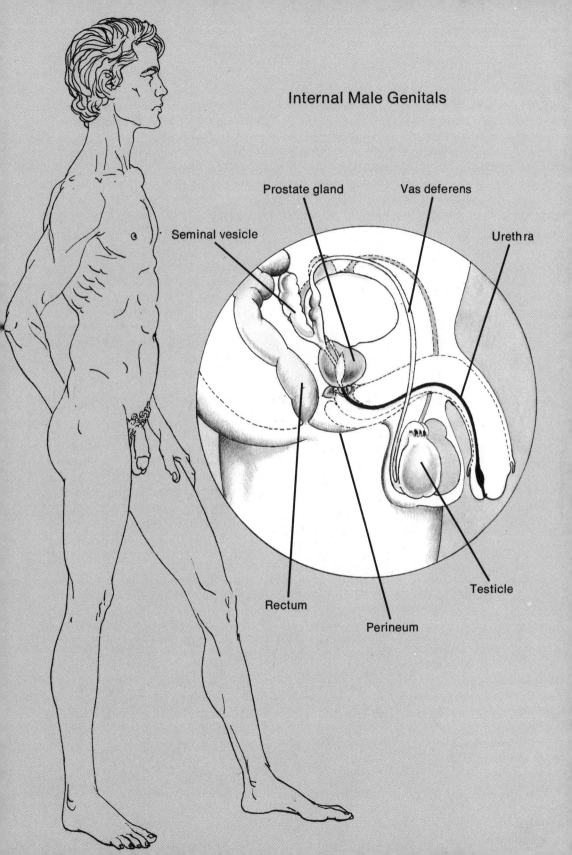

Internal Male Genitals

Seminal vesicle

Prostate gland

Vas deferens

Urethra

Rectum

Perineum

Testicle

- *There are men with penises too big to fit your vagina.* Nonsense: The vagina is elastic tissue and can stretch to fit anyone but the Jolly Green Giant!

Surprise! Surprise! Did You Know That . . . ? (And These Things Are All *True!*)
- *The average penis can double in size in three seconds.* That's as long as it takes you to say "Yes!"
- *The length and width of the penis is variable.* Penises range from two to six inches in length, and from one to two inches in width at rest. During erection, the penis may be anywhere from four to nine inches in length, up to two and a half inches in width. Stop measuring!
- *Men's nipples become tingly and erect during sex* (just like yours!)
- *Nearly one hundred percent of the male population has masturbated extensively.* And in a great variety of styles. Some men caress their members lightly, others pull and stroke strenuously. Most let go during ejaculation.
- *Some men have such sensitive penises that the tip hurts if it remains in the vagina after ejaculation.*
- *Many men plunge their penises deep into your vagina during the spasmodic seconds of orgasm.*
- *One-day-old male babies and eighty-nine-year-old men can have erections.* Neither of these two should interest you.

Now, here's what happens when a man becomes aroused. Sex impulses start in his brain (from thinking about something sexy—say, *you*) and in his genitals (from being touched). These impulses travel along nerves to an erection nerve-center near the base of his spine. (Remember how important we told you that area is?) The stimulation causes blood to rush into his penis, which grows hard, longer, thicker, and erect. (The medical term is vasocongestion.) *Voilà!*

𝒜 man with an erection may not always be interested in having sex with you. His erection can also mean:
- He just woke up. (Many men's penises rise when they do in the morning—part of the dreaming process, not necessarily sexually connected.)
- He just lifted a heavy object (not you).
- He's constipated and has been straining.
- He has some physical ailment, most likely a urinary problem.

Your man's erection can vanish as quickly as it appeared, particularly if it is the authentic passion erection. The man is gearing toward sex, and any antisex stimulation will make him lose desire. The penis can become flaccid if:

- There is a sudden, loud noise. (Your phone rings.)
- You mention something unsexy: "You're double-parked outside. I hope you don't get a ticket."
- The lights suddenly go on.
- The lights suddenly go off.
- There is a draft.
- Your (his) mother enters the room.

Assuming none of these catastrophes happens (and in Chapter Nine, we'll tell you how to *avoid* disaster), the lover stays erect.

*W*hat happens then? Dr. William H. Masters and Dr. Virginia E. Johnson, the sex researchers, observed men (and women) at all stages of sexual response and monitored their vital signs. (How these men and women made love with cameras, electrodes, and doctors hanging about I'll *never* know— but the doctors did record the findings, and published them in a book called *Human Sexual Response*.) Thanks to them, we now know *exactly* what happens during sexual activity.

After much kissing and stroking on your part (or masturbation on his own part), his muscles tense, his penis becomes bigger, redder (maybe even a bit purplish). If *extremely* excited, he may show a red rash—called sexual flush—on his stomach and chest. The penis is erect and looks as if it will stay that way (more or less—doctors report some wavering.)

Then with continued excitement, the rash, if there is one, deepens, nipples become taut, the heart pounds as high as 100–175 beats a minute. (Normal rate is 86.) Blood pressure rises, too. The penis becomes still larger and deeper in color. His testicles may enlarge as much as fifty percent over their usual size. There's a decreased supply of blood to the brain, a straining for breath.

Now nerve impulses reach his ejaculation nerve-center near the base of his spine. He has recurring contractions of the *sphincter urethrae, bulbo-spongiosus, ischiocavernosus,* and *transverse superficial and deep perineal muscles.* All *that* need mean to you is his whole penis is quivering and shaking with internal spasms. These spasms start at the rate of an .08th of a second, then slow down. They force the seminal fluid through the urethra and out the tip of the penis. The spurts become weaker. His breath is short and fast. Ejaculation is over.

At this point, he might perspire profusely from his palms to the soles of his feet. A lethargy sets in. There is no inclination to talk . . . or move. His penis begins to retract and becomes flaccid again. This detumescence can be quite sudden or (if the sex was particularly good or long-lasting) proceed more slowly. Masters and Johnson say detumescence happens at "varying and arbitrary rates" in different men under different circumstances. The length of time needed before he can have *another* erection also varies. Most men usually need some rest and often manual or oral stimulation, too, before they become excited again.

So you see, the male sexual response is somewhat simpler and *briefer* than your own. Your heart pounds harder, your vaginal contractions last longer than his penis spasms. And you can have repeated orgasms if stimulation is continued, while the man's ejaculation is a single, shorter experience *that is not necessarily orgasmic.*

No, ejaculation is not the same as orgasm. With all the talk and research about helping women achieve orgasms more often than they do, we find it sad that not much attention has been paid to helping *men* have more orgasmic experiences. Masters and Johnson believe this gap is caused by society's concentration on male *erection, performance, prowess,* rather than the deep physical and psychological ecstasy that *women* seek. Some men do occasionally experience something close to a woman's orgasmic pleasure, a "feminine" orgasm more exquisite and prolonged than the short spasm of his usual finale. This is the ultimate fulfillment for your man— as it is for you—and we will show you later how to help him toward it.

*Losing your
virginity—without
losing your cool*

EIGHT

Be forewarned! Orgasmic bliss will not be yours the very first time. You may love the man, he may be a darling, his technique may be smooth as velvet . . . and still the experience is likely to be slightly painful, a bit messy, and probably nonorgasmic.

Two-thirds of all girls start with a hymen—a little membrane that partially blocks the entrance to the vagina. Even if your hymen has survived childhood acrobatics, early experiences with tampons, and later heavy petting, it might give you minor trouble during your first sex act. The man's penis will have to tear or stretch the hymen. You will bleed a little and maybe hurt a little. You *can* prepare for the first time by asking a doctor to surgically deflower you in his office. He will give you a topical anesthetic, then cut or stretch the hymen. You may bleed a little, and for a day or two, a vaginal discharge will float away the excess tissue. The doctor will also give you a dilator, with simple instructions for using it to stretch the opening a few minutes a day for a short while. (Otherwise the healthy tissues would close up again.)

One-third of all women, however, don't have this inconvenient membrane and will experience *none* of the extra fuss—but probably won't see *fireworks*, either. Sex takes some getting used to . . . and the first act is a very emotional experience as well as a physical one. Many girls make unfortunate scenes in bed. You *needn't!*

Things not to do when losing your virginity:
  • beg him to tell you he loves you*
  • cry hysterically*

* Don't commit these sexual *faux pas* later on, either, with any man—on any night!
page 115

- scream*
- fake multiple orgasms*
- ask "Is this your first time, too?"
- demand to be taken to a doctor
- ask if you are constructed like other girls*

For your first sexual experience, you want a skilled, considerate lover—not a drunk or a salesman passing through town. But the ideal deflowerer need *not* be the man who makes you see colored lights when he says "Hi, honey." A surfeit of romantic expectations is probably the number one source of sexual disillusionment. *Some* girls have even discovered—after the fact—that they were lucky to lose their virginity with a former childhood buddy who happened to be in town that weekend, or a notorious womanizer who happily, kindly shared his confident expertise for one night. A sexual bungler is not much fun no matter how much you love him, and two people losing their virginity together is usually six times as uninteresting as one at a time.

To be fair to the man (who may have queasy thoughts about virgins), tell him: You are a virgin, but don't want to stay one. You are eager to learn. You like him and want him to be your first lover.

If he balks, find another man. Men who really don't want the role shouldn't have to play it. There will be many willing men in the wings.

Every girl loses her virginity differently. Some girls are forced. Others passionately seduce their first lovers. Still other girls have sex almost by "accident." Because each experience is different, we thought you'd benefit most from another girl's experiences with two (yes, *two*) kinds of deflowering:

Getting Deflowered the Second Time Around
For exactly half my life I was a virgin. I was seventeen when I made the conscious decision to dispose of those few inches and inhibitions that kept me an innocent . . . pretty ignorant of what precisely went on when a man stopped being a "boyfriend" and became a "lover."

The experience should have been celestial. It had all the ingredients for a romantic deflowering. The man was thirty. I had met him two days before aboard the ship taking me on my first trip to Europe. He was French. He had blue eyes. It was a calm night at sea. I was not nervous because he was so obviously experienced, and I knew that deep down I was sexy, only waiting for that wonderful moment that would release more pleasure than

I had ever known. How many times before had I stopped short of the final act because the man wasn't right, the mood wasn't right! But we were two blissful days out at sea; this man was older, and, of course, he was French!

It was awful.

For the next six years of my life I was convinced something was wrong with me, something subtle and unclassified in any of the books on sexology I read so avidly. I lied to each subsequent man I went to bed with. I told him it was marvelous; yet, even when I had an orgasm, sex *wasn't* really marvelous. Something was missing. I lied to my girl friends, too, when they talked about the agony and the ecstasy of making love. I felt like a cheat whenever I flirted with men at parties, knowing that although I dressed and behaved with extreme seductiveness, I simply was *not* a complete woman. I even lied once to a Kinsey-style investigator who interviewed me.

"Oh sure," I told her. "I always have an orgasm. I really *like* sex." It wasn't true. Ashamed to tell anyone else, I had to admit to *myself* that I was destined to endure a sort of low-key frigidity, a condition I summed up as "chilly." Although I was plenty *active* sexually, there were at best just a few moments of sharp pleasure in the sex act for me, often not even that. Into my early twenties I was pretty certain I would never hear the bells nor feel *anything* for a man beyond a savage crush, a need, sometimes a jealousy. I felt I would never experience the magic that can truly join two people in love and in bed.

Of course, what I didn't realize at the time was that in everything but one technical detail I was still a virgin.

When I was twenty-three, I met—and subsequently went to bed with— a man who was not unlike men I had met and bedded before. At twenty-eight, he was good-looking but not spectacular, kind but not totally unselfish, clever but not a genius. He was, in short, another nice man, and I began the affair because I enjoyed his company, also because I thought I *should* go to bed with him; certainly I had done my best to make sure he wanted (badly) to go to bed with *me*. Sleeping with him turned out to be pleasant enough, and sometimes, almost by accident it seemed, I had the famous orgasm. Nevertheless, a part of me just wasn't *there*, a part of me was detached, unused, pure. It could have been the sixtieth time with this lover, or maybe the sixty-third, when I finally stopped being a virgin . . . for the second time.

I didn't lose my second virginity in bed or on a sofa; I lost it on the far side of the room from him. He was standing, looking out of a window, and I had been reading a newspaper. I glanced up, looked at him, and for the first time in my life I lusted . . . a wave of honest sexual desire nearly smothered me, and I wanted him in a passionate way I had never realized a woman could want a man. Right then I told him I wanted him, and, in the rush of his genuine delight and my spontaneous hunger, my virginity was at last washed away.

I was never a virgin again, neither with him nor, after we parted, with any other man. Yes, we did separate eventually, realizing that we were not in love; but I *cared* about him and still do. He was the man who finally allowed me to stop being a virgin.

*P*erhaps any man at that moment could have spun me into orbit. Perhaps the time had come to open my mind to the knowledge that the sexual act is made of mutual desire—not just his for me, or even mine for him, but ours for each other. Until that point, I had simply done my best to be desirable, kept myself as polished as a glossy shell, but had forgotten all about what I was really *for* or really wanted. I had presented myself as a sexy object and looked around for a man to take me, all of me, but never had I understood that nothing could be taken *from* me, not even my virginity; it could only be given by me freely to the man I wanted to have it. The sexual act, I learned, was not something performed upon me like a tattoo or a massage, but an act to which I had to contribute desire, spontaneity, honesty, in order to harvest my own pleasure. Sex was a ritual in which I had to participate with the movements of my body and to which I must surrender enthusiastically those last, lingering vanities and inhibitions that can be called second virginity. My reward for offering this second virginity with a whole heart was more than just orgasm—even virgins can have *those*. It was a contentment and satisfaction, a kind of arrival that I had never let myself know before in the arms of a man.

There can't be any rule about losing one's second virginity, the *essential* virginity, any more than there are rules about losing the first one . . . the *technical* virginity. My own profound second deflowering happened when I was ready for it and when I was with a man who, although not one of the world's famous lovers, was a responsive, sensitive person.

I was lucky. Some of my friends are still waiting—in a state of alarmed frustration—for that proverbial great lover . . . that fabulous prince who will trigger them over the threshold of their own sexuality into a state of perfect bliss. They talk wistfully about finding a man with real *technique*, a sort of tender engineer who will set in motion their deepest happiness. I suppose they think he will push mysterious buttons and make it all happen; yet, to my mind, a man's lovemaking technique is at least half within the control of his partner. Any woman who is still essentially a virgin, still waiting to be pushed into womanhood, will probably not be liberated enough or bold enough to show her lover how to give her pleasure. She waits, impatient but passive, for an impossible paragon to deliver this carefree joy in bed, which, ironically, he cannot possibly accomplish without her help. But she will remain too shy, too *virginal* in fact, to experiment . . . to tell him what pleases her.

I know a man who is a lover of some reputation, celebrated for his skillful conquests, his physical prowess ("My dear, he can last all *night*"), but I have never envied any of his mistresses. Although he supposedly can read a woman's body like a street map, his relationships have never been long or happy ones. To achieve this reputation as a lover with great technique, a man must remain *detached* from his partner who, in turn, becomes just another body to him; he must be completely absorbed in his *own* performance. Probably a man like this who is *known* for his performance (and there have been one or two world-famous ones) is *himself* an essential virgin; he will never have lowered his own resistance enough to become spontaneous and human.

"Every time I go to bed with a woman," a friendly Don Juan once told me (as if to prove my thesis), "I'm a virgin again. And in the morning I'm *still* a virgin. I keep trying to lose it once and for all, and if I ever do, I'll stay with that woman for the rest of my life. As it is, I meet girls I've been to bed with, and I can't remember anything about them, as if the affair never happened. Every time is the first time, and every time is a disappointment in a funny sort of way."

Many women have come so hopefully to this kind of man, trusting him to lead them into full womanhood. Sadly they don't realize he hasn't yet *himself* learned that it's in the humanity of lovemaking, in the connection of two people who are, at least for the moment, perfectly satisfied together, that virginity is melted. Nonvirginity is really a way of thinking about sex that can come to you all on your own when there is no lover around, as well as in the arms of someone you allow yourself to be happy with.

I can't believe any woman is capable of giving herself totally and without inhibitions to a man she doesn't find attractive, although many, including myself, have given their second virginity to a man with whom they were not deeply in *love*. Fortunately, we don't all find the same men irresistible, and, fortunately again, one woman can find pleasure with a man where other women have failed. Two of my friends have been to bed with the same man. One of them told me that although she was fond of him, he left her cold sexually. "It didn't work in bed. I never felt relaxed." The other girl says that if she were not so jealous, she would lend this same man to each of her friends so they could all enjoy "his wonderful presence in bed." I guess the point I am trying to make is that no lover is in bed by *himself,* nor is his partner; before *he* can become a lover, before *she* can become a lover, they must each have someone else in that bed . . . each other!

And the combination of one man with one woman is never quite the same as the combination of that man with some *other* woman. Tony with Sara was not the same Tony who made love to Janet. Janet wanted him and Sara felt restrained. Maybe Sara had good reasons for her reservations: maybe Tony was too intense for her, or maybe there was a physical aspect to their union she didn't dare tell him offended her. Or possibly Sara was not quite ready to surrender to *any* man. Maybe she is still waiting to be bullied and shoved into a state of joy which she doesn't know how to enter voluntarily. This is certainly not to say that Sara is frigid; like me and, I suspect, like millions of other women, she will probably surrender her reservations when the time, the place, the partner, and her own way of thinking about sex are ripe.

It would be splendid if we could all be sure our ideas about sex would, in time, become less virginal; but sexual maturity isn't easily achieved. My grandmother admits that even in the embraces of her marriage she felt guilty if she found too much pleasure. The quality of feminine guilt has changed, but the guilt still exists, and a woman who feels any shame about making love retains her basic virginity! That's one of the problems. Although there are fewer technical virgins around these days, there are just as many *essential* virgins. We are nowadays taught to *seek* pleasure and practically ordered to find rapture in sex if we want to be called normal.

Yet a modern woman, earning her own (good) money, driving her own car, definitely living her own life, can actually still feel guilty if she likes sex, with the added problem of feeling *equally* guilty if she doesn't like it at all! There may be an orgasm in sex for any woman, but if that pleasure is followed by remorse, the sexual act is then tarnished; it becomes more and more tense, more and more an act of virginal masturbation. "I have a hot bath the next morning and forget it ever happened," a friend of mine once said, speaking of her many escapades. Although she insisted she was a liberated woman "without any inhibitions," sexual pleasure for the *genuine* nonvirgin is clearly something to remember, not something to forget. That this particular girl was simply a virgin-on-the-Pill, *still* guilt-ridden and shy, became clear even to her when she finally established a long, tender relationship with a man she fell in love with and later married.

For her and for many other women, only true love and marriage finally erode the guilt they feel for giving themselves fully to the sexual act. Ideal though the notion may be of saving the true self for a man who is truly loved, the woman who does this risks disappointment. She may give her husband her *physical* virginity and still find herself unable to give him *everything,* unable to free herself from the drab inheritance tainting even *our* permissive generation—the belief that the sexual act is dirty and fraught with peril. To demolish the inhibitions of an essential virgin, love is not always enough; it takes time, too, and patience.

I knew a girl who waited for both love and marriage before giving up any part of her virginity . . . waited with dignity and with admirable control while all her friends were busy experimenting in the arms of lovers. Six years ago she married the man she loved, but, contrary to what we all expected, marriage didn't suit her. She grew haggard and irritable, developed the mannerisms of a disappointed woman. "It's not what I thought it would be" was all she would tell me when I talked with her about a year after the wedding. Last month I saw her for the first time in years, and she was blooming. "What a baby I was" she said. "I don't know what happened, but this last year has been marvelous." Then, with a new frankness, she told me how she had finally learned in time the pleasure of sex, had stopped waiting for something wonderful to be done to her, and had decided to "do something wonderful." She had learned how to express love with her body and how to get for both her husband and herself the most pleasure possible from their sex life. Several years after being deflowered, she had finally gotten rid of her virginity! "I never had imagined," she said, "that making love could be much *fun.* I used to take it so seriously in the beginning."

*A*side from guilt, there are clinging, vague fears that can keep a woman from pleasure and lock her up inside her own virginal psyche. A very elegant, successful forty-year-old (technical) virgin is far along the way to becoming an old maid. In her deluxe New York apartment she once told me, "I have always been afraid I wouldn't be any *good* at sex." Fear has kept this particular woman a virgin in *every* way, and it is fear that keeps many other women *essential* virgins . . . virgins in their souls. Fear of losing *themselves,* fear of ridicule, fear of involvement, fear of not being good in bed even though they look seductive. I even know one girl who was afraid that if she allowed herself to enjoy the sex act she might like it so much she would become promiscuous, although promiscuous women are often the most desperate, hard-core virgins of them all! Fears disappear with time, with experience, with love, or with all three. If I couldn't laugh now at most of the things I have feared in the past, I'd become catatonic and go sit in a corner.

The real *non*virgin knows herself and her lover better in the morning than she did the night before, for she has stopped being afraid she will never find that special mate and can look kindly at the man she is with. She likes men more than a virgin does because she sees them as *people*, not as miracle workers. Men usually like *her*, too. For the nonvirgin, sex is stimulating, clean, and, above all, fun! Of course, the harder you work at having fun, the farther away it goes; and sex, if you work too hard, can become a perpetual New Year's Eve party that doesn't quite get off the ground. In order to be fun, the sex act calls for some inspiration . . . a temperamental quality that refuses to be summoned whenever we want it. But inspiration will come of its own sweet accord when least expected, when we are most relaxed, when we are no longer quite so young, perhaps, or hung up on ourselves as objects to be desired, when we are willing to contribute our desirability *and* our desires, our personalities and our bodies, our wit and our joy to the man at our side and to the most delightful game that two can play.

*That first
night with a
new man*

NINE

You want him; he wants you. Now you're going to have each other. And this prelude time is most *jittery*. You churn with desire—but also quiver with "first night nerves." Will he turn out to be the lover you wanted? Will he like your naked body? Will your love styles coalesce? Or, horrors, will there be an awkward fumble in the dark, an ashamed, sour silence afterward? A myriad of things could ruin the night, a thousand trivialities interfere with what might be your loveliest love experience. When sex goes badly, there can be nothing *worse*—your bodies move out of sync with the rhythms of love, you are left with an emotional hangover that can depress you for months.

Cheer up! *Everyone* has such fears . . . usually unfounded. And you *can* plan ahead to foil all the little contingencies that might interfere with a fabulous night of love.

Beforehand—that's the key to successful first nights. Cope with potential problems—roommates, relatives, pets, visitors, ringing telephones, convertible sofas, hairpieces, and heaven knows *what* else (we'll *tell* you!)— *before* they ruin your evening.

The Advance-Planning Principle: Rules for Minimizing Nasty Variables That Could Wreck the Evening
Rule One: As soon as you have decided that you *do* want to sleep with this man (we assume *he* wants *you!*), plan for the occasion. Forget spontaneity for this first sexual encounter. The fantasy of your newfound lover throwing you down in a field of daisies sounds exciting, but in reality, there's poison ivy among the flowers, and three farmhands and a Boy Scout troop witness your amours. Plan. Plan.

Rule Two: Steer the action to your place, where you'll have the advantage of familiarity. Here you know the way to the bathroom, how to turn on the stereo—no strange hallways or unflattering fluorescent lights. You can sneak off for makeup repairs, control exits and entrances. Most vital plus: the psychological advantage of feeling comfortable and at home will make you *confident*—even when you're secretly *scared!*

Rule Three: Make sure you will not be disturbed! Create a romantic, erotic mood and don't let *anything* destroy it! We'll tell you how . . . but first things first.

Your Body: How to Keep It from Exerting a Will of Its Own

You are nervous. When you are nervous, you perspire . . . more than usual. Use the toughest antiperspirant in the business, the one that's practically all aluminum and *really* lasts for hours. Natalie Wood is said to *swear* by Mitchum's for really *serious* circumstances (say, under red-hot TV lights); you may find a less potent product fine for red-hot *private* appearances.

Just when you need your body most, it lets you down. First-night jitters often produce hives, blemishes, bad breath (the kind that strikes no matter *how* clean your mouth is—comes from nervous tummy!) Your glands are working overtime, curse them. Keep your face scrupulously lean. Use a medicated makeup if you're prone to emotional breakouts. Watch your diet. Don't eat a heavy lunch or dinner on *the* day. For stomachaches and related tension, take an alkaline soother (a liquid, like Pepto Bismol, or a tablet, like Tums). That should also help your breath. Add a mask of mints (preferably sugar-free) or a breath spray.

Mood Maintenance: Coping with an Unerotic Environment

Roommates or Relatives Who Live with You

We told you to live alone! But, if you are living at home or with friends, don't worry, we won't abandon you. There *is* this housing shortage, after all, and you may *have* to share with another girl. We *do* suggest that if the other girl is your *mother,* you tryst elsewhere (unless she happens to be *totally* uninhibited, in which case, treat her as you would a roommate). If you are living in an Ozzie-and-Harriet family setup, forget sex at home . . . live in, love out.

Do try to have a roommate who works nights or is out of town often. Such "absentee" roommates include: airline stewardesses, traveling saleswomen, touring actresses, girls who are really living with men but need someplace to keep their clothes. If you can't find an absentee roommate, try for one who works nights: nurse, cocktail waitress, Playboy bunny, exotic dancer, night bank clerk, night cleaning lady (who may also keep things nice and tidy for you during the day).

All right, you already *have* a roommate—a comrade who works during the day and hangs around relentlessly from five to bedtime. You *can* offer inducements (movie, theater tickets) to get her out of the apartment on crucial nights. Always tell her *why* you need the apartment (to make love with Jim). Lying is unfair and *dangerous*. (Mary Jane may burst in to get her alligator shoes.) She must stay out *all* night!

Never try to make love while Mary Jane is still around (unless you two share a fifteen-room mansion). Mary Jane may get jealous, and besides, it's just plain unromantic to make love while someone in the next room is yukking it up at *Laugh-In* or doing calisthenics.

Cats, Dogs, Talking Birds, and Other Beasts
Don't let pets intrude on your sex life. Lover may panic if Rover or Puss pounces on the bed while you're making love. Also, as one animal-lover friend put it, "It's hard to feel sexy when a cocker spaniel with a rubber bone in his mouth is watching you." Some dogs may lunge for the throat of the "stranger" who appears to be attacking you. So keep pets in another room—unless you'll then have to listen to an animal whimpering, whining, barking, meowing, or scraping at the door. In *that* case, better remove pet from the premises, leave with friends or a kennel. Better still—retrain your animal to sit docilely in a room by himself. (Try not to have too many pets . . . he'll think you *only* like the animal kind!)

Don't keep a talking bird near your bed. No matter how often you've seen this erotic touch in nineteenth-century paintings of odalisques, it's so *terribly* impractical that I can't believe those painters were ever *in* an odalisque's bedroom! Parrots and parakeets tend to squawk and flap their wings when they sense that the action is lively. Let Polly mutter to herself in a distant corner, spew her seeds and fruit peels elsewhere.

Turtles, lizards, goldfish, and other cold-blooded creatures are silent and don't interfere. They should not be *loose,* however.

Monkeys and other simians prove near-to-impossible to control, and are so humanlike they make one feel uncomfortable. So you may have to make a choice: Tarzan or Cheetah?

Visitors
Tell everyone you know that you're going out of town. If the door buzzer rings, don't answer. If you have next-door neighbors who come knocking,

don't answer for them either. Even in tower apartment houses some folksy neighbors may open the door and cry, "Yoo-hoo—anybody home?" Lock the door as soon as you and your man are inside.

Ringing Telephones

Just as the two of you move passionately to the bed, the phone rings. This *may* affect him physically (cause him to lose his erection) . . . it will *certainly* shatter the mood. Did you know that you can turn *off* the bell on a standard telephone? Just look at the underside of the phone. There is a dial. Push it all the way over to "low" (usually toward the left), and the ring won't be very audible.

Taking the receiver off the hook is a much less sensible strategy. On some phones, loud, beeping noises ensue to remind you of your tactic. Also, the one time I tried this, about fifteen people called, got a busy signal, decided I must be home, and all came over and rang the doorbell. My *mother* called and decided the phone was busy for so long that I must be in some danger—passed out from gas while trying to reach the police, perhaps. So she sent a *telegram* and . . . oh, believe me, taking the receiver off the hook is a *terrible* idea.

Clunking Appliances

Ecstasy is within reach . . . then your dishwasher enters its *clunka-clunka-boom-boom* cycle. Don't run appliances while your man is with you, unless you like their rhythm.

The Bed . . . And How to Make It

Should you make the bed beforehand? Or wait until you are almost upon it? If your bed is in a real (separate) bedroom, prepare it ahead of time—just sheets, pillow, and (depending on the weather) a blanket or comforter for later coziness. But if the bed sits in an alcove or in your living room, the ready-to-slide-between-the-sheets look can unnerve a man who arrives to take you to dinner and finds himself staring at mauve percale from the moment he enters the room. Beds that are in view should be covered with a spread (fur throws are expensive, but super . . . but never use fur from a threatened species!) You can kick the spread off whenever you choose.

The convertible sofa is a popular choice for studio-apartment dwellers, but poses its own unique problem: When do you convert the convertible? Before the man arrives? No, better wait . . . the converted sofa will turn a tiny studio into a wall-to-wall bed (fine for later, but not for an entrance). There's no way to convert a sofa *passionately*. ("Here, honey—toss these cushions over there, while I yank up on the mattress.") Suggestion: Convert the sofa *after* lovemaking, make love the first time on the floor. This can be a *plus* if the floor is covered by shaggy rugs or fake fur skins. Once the first throes of passion are spent, you can nonchalantly convert the sofa and purr happily away on it later.

I think it's only fair to warn you, though, that some forms of sexual liberation have not seeped into the consciousnesses of some men . . . and it is *possible* that your man will never have made love on a floor, may feel you are too "aggressive" (perhaps even a "bad girl") for suggesting this delightful idea. Many girls have found their own enjoyment of sexuality met with *shock* by men who can't quite get used to the idea that sexual freedom is for *both* sexes. Over the long haul, that's a problem for women's (and men's) liberation . . . but what do you do with this particular man in your apartment right *now?*

As far as the floor goes, if he expresses dismay or reluctance, you might as well convert the bed. It's not all *that* mood-destroying! One (admittedly rather sophisticated) man I knew said he *loved* to watch me convert the bed . . . he thought it rather *endearing!* (I later rewarded him by making sure the *real* bed I eventually bought was extra long to accommodate him.) However, the unliberated man who freaks out about love on the floor may well prove to have problems in *other* areas, too. You'll have to deal with these as they arise, decide how much you *really* want to be involved with a man who may secretly think sex is just a little *loathesome.*

Temperature Control
Lovemaking in warm weather can get sticky. Turn the air conditioner on *hours* before you think you'll need it. No air conditioner? Try a window fan . . . cooling breezes add an interesting special effect as your nightgown billows and your hair blows across your face.

Cold weather can be dealt with more simply: Cuddle up, keep moving.

Fireplaces
If you have a working fireplace, let it work while you make love. The symbolism of the crackling flames, shooting sparks, need not be explained. (Remember Tony Perkins and Melina Mercouri making love in front of a fire in *Phaedra?*) Do, however, set your fire beforehand: arrange paper, kindling, and split logs. Then, at the crucial moment, ask him to light a match and let the passions blaze. Be sure you use *wood*—paper logs, milk cartons, shirt cardboards, just don't have the same effect.

Sound Effects ·
Don't *hope* the radio will play something crashingly sexual—you'll end up listening to a revival of 1940's novelty tunes. Stack records that turn *you* on . . . thereby influencing the mood and tempo of the action by controlling the music. (See page 77 for suggestions.) If you *must* depend on a radio, steer clear of the commercial stations . . . unless you want to make love to a gasoline jingle. Turn to FM, long-listening programs.

Love Snacks
Keep an iced pitcher of your lover's favorite drink in the refrigerator. Frost glasses by washing them (don't dry), then placing them in freezer for a few minutes.

Little snack-foods won't mess the bed. (No lasagna unless he sees it in the refrigerator and hankers for some.) Slices of icy-fresh organically grown fruit and raw vegetables quench your lover's thirst . . . so do grapes, the traditional erotic tidbit, fun to feed to each other! In addition to those non-perishables we advised you to lay in *permanently* (see page 99, you might stock some hearty rye or pumpernickel, mustard, and mayonnaise (for sandwiches), just in case he gets *really* ravenous for more than *you*. Of course, if you *know* he has a special pet craving (one man I knew was mad for yogurt in bed), you *will* cater to it, won't you?

Don't try to *cook* in the midst of a romantic "first night." That will come later. In Chapter Eleven we'll tell you all you need to nourish a man through an affair.) Tonight, relax!

Sex Supplies
Keep a few pleasure-enhancers discreetly at bedside or in a nearby drawer: fresh towels, friction rub, massage cream, decanter of sherry.

How to Take Off Your Clothes
The stage is set. You have prepared a wonderful environment conducive to love, coped with potential problems. But a critical stage of first-night sex still may worry you. Everybody is eager to advise you how to dress . . . but does anyone tell you how to *undress?* How to shed your clothes seductively? Should you run to the bathroom and emerge naked? In a peignoir? Does that "slip-into-something-more-comfortable" cliché still work? Or should you just lie there and let *him* undress you?

If you undress with flair, you can accomplish all these objectives:
- Arouse the man.
- Stimulate yourself.

- Get rid of your clothes, hairpieces, and any other prosthetic devices that won't stand the rigors of sex. (Actually, though, we would advise you to encumber yourself with as few of the latter as possible—especially the first time you make love with a man. It's only *later* in a relationship that a man is likely to say, as one did about my friend Nancy, "I love to see her take off her false eyelashes—she looks so *vulnerable* without them." That sort of sentiment comes from sustained love and affection that has grown over some period of time. On your *first* encounter with a man, you want him to see you at your best . . . and removing a barrage of beauty aids is disillusioning as well as a nuisance.)

Review: Remember—your body is clean, soft, and sweet-smelling. You've bathed, used lotions, perfume, powder. Hair you don't want is gone. Your birth control method is in effect. Onward!

$\mathcal{N}$ow, your underwear. Does it enhance your beautiful body? Plain Jane Doe cotton doesn't. Using your intuition, select a style of underwear that you think will set off your looks, excite him:
- french frills on a boyish figure
- pristine white or midnight black against a glowing tan
- pink to give a rosy illumination to sallow skin
- naughty see-through if he usually sees you in the office

Men love pretty colors as much as *you* do. Save the designer prints for elsewhere, though; they may impress other women. The focal point is *you,* not a high-fashion designer. Never disrobe and unveil:
- a girdle (ugh!) (If you're plump, hang loose—think you're a Renoir nude, a Maillol woman.)
- armor-type brassiere (Wear a sexy bra or none at all.)
- garters digging into your thighs
- red impressions from tight elastic waistbands or straps (Bikini panties and hip-high pantyhose won't leave marks unless they're too tight.)

Keep the mechanics simple. Your clothes should be easy to remove—no elaborate clasp and fastener arrangements. (Most of the really natural-looking bras have no fastener at all; they stretch so you can step in and out of them or lift them over your head.) The best *un*dresses can be dropped in a second: wraparounds (just untie and let fall), caftans (pull over head, toss aside), single-zipper dresses (unzip, step out). Men seem to like dresses with zip-fronts, which they can playfully pull open—down your cleavage and beyond.

New fashion trends make undressing easier than ever before. (Aren't you *glad?*) Some kicky frocks have *no* closings—elastic waists stretch, dress can be flipped over the head. Other little-nothing halter-top styles simply tie at the back of the neck. Wear one of these frisky dresses. The first night is no time to sport a layered look or a gown that closes with eighty-five seed pearl buttons.

*S*hould you allow *him* to take control of your undressing? Some men *love* to remove your clothes (and love *you* to remove *theirs!*) Styles vary: One man may unbutton you tenderly, as if you were a helpless little girl; another may take an almost fiendish pleasure in stripping you with a single stroke. If you *do* let the man undress you, be willing to risk an impatiently ripped seam, a four-hundred-dollar St. Laurent white midi dropped carelessly on the floor. (Above all, don't shoot the poor man a black look, grab the treasure, and rush off to place it on its padded hanger!) If you *care* that he might ruin your clothes, say gently, "Let *me*," and disrobe your way.

There are *other* real advantages to doing the striptease yourself. First, you can handle the disrobing more skillfully and gracefully. You can also stand in soft, flattering light. (The *man* might pull your dress off in the stark arena of the kitchen.) With dramatic flair, you can disclose your best features first, de-emphasize your flaws. (If your hips are floppy, reveal them last—show your pert, pretty breasts *first*.)

Move *gracefully* when you undress, enjoy showing your nice body in action instead of cringing and skulking over to the bedcovers. Look into his eyes, watch his responses. Here are some evocative striptease motions:
- Lift dress high over your head with a long, lazy stretch. (This pushes your breasts high, tightens midriff muscles.)
- Bend languorously as you roll off your stockings or pantyhose.
- Arch backward to reach down for a shoe, or take them off sitting down, lifting each leg high in the air à la Dietrich.
- Lie down—then lift your legs, point them high, ease out of your panties.
- Slip your panties off while you're still in a dress.
- Hold a dress in front of you after you've taken it off. Then drop it. (*Don't* rush to hang it up . . . drop it over a *chair* if you'll really *worry* about it.)

- Undress with a light at your back. (You will appear as a supple silhouette.)

How to Look Great in the Nude
Now that you're undressed, do you feel stripped and helpless? Haven't you always wanted someone to tell you how to look *better* in the nude? There *are* techniques to help you look your naked best, tell you what to do about droop breasts, chicken chest, ripple thighs, that old appendectomy scar, washboard behind . . . all the bare facts you've had to cope with alone till now.

No, we're *not* going to give you another lecture on diet and exercise to improve your figure. You already *know* you should do those things, and *someday* you will. But, meanwhile, you have to face a new lover *tonight*—and you're five or ten pounds overweight, or your thighs are flabby. Don't panic, we're not going to leave you standing there. Here are the emergency tactics to use tonight, if you must!

You don't have to be built like Ursula Andress to look ravishing in the buff. All you need is a little know-how and confidence to ward off that vulnerable plucked-chicken feeling—all gooseflesh and poking drumsticks. Now, take these cosmetic steps toward seductive nudity:
- Analyze your skin type. Are you pale? sultry? sallow?
- List your pluses—pretty breasts?—and your minuses—fat stomach? Remember what other men have *liked* about your body.

If you've followed our earlier instructions, your room is softly lit. A warm, rosy glow will play over your body. If your skin is really greenish, bring up rosiness with redder bulbs. If you're too ruddy (happens to blondes and redheads), cool the lights with a soft blue bulb. Use the same flattering tones for your skin type on the bed linens. Pink sheets will warm the most yellow skin, yellow or cool green will work the opposite effect. If your body skin is freckled, blotched, or veiny, dim the lights even lower. Remember to keep light at your *back*—not glaring down upon you. Other remedies for faulty flesh tones:
- leg makeup—for the worst spots (like varicose veins)
- a honey-brown tan—by sun, sun lamp, or bronzing stick
- a hot bath just before he arrives—turns skin pink
- fifteen minutes of rugged exercise just before striptease (if you're spending weekend in country or at beach), to make blood rush to surface and promote a healthy blush

Okay, the flesh tones are cleared up. Now, *what* can you do about those hulking three-dimensional figure flaws? First, take stock of yourself. Your whole *body* isn't a single flaw! Think how nice your breasts or your buttocks are. And remember: No one's perfect, not even Raquel Welch. (*She* has stretch marks.) Feel proud of your good points; take these corrective measures for the following conditions:

Droop Breasts
Description: Breasts are too large or flaccid to perk up on their own. Gravity wins, and they land somewhere at waist level, or dangle like little empty beanbags. With breasts like this, you look fine (maybe even *great*) in clothes and bras, but the minute you undress, everything flops. *Cure:* Undress while lying down. In the supine position (that's on your *back*), breasts won't appear to fall. Even huge mammaries tilt upward, look terrific. Of course, eventually, you'll have to stand up . . . but not until *much, much* later. And then you can cross your arms under your breasts (the "human bra" maneuver). Keep shoulders back to get the most support from your chest muscles. There is also some very sexy body jewelry, like pearl vests, chain halters, that could work for you.

Flat Chest
Description: Your breasts don't droop—you're just flat as a pancake. *Cure:* When you stand or walk, press the sides of your upper arms slightly against your chest to squeeze in some cleavage. Bend over *often*—you'll look supple and divine. And *do* confront your man head-on—you won't look so flat as in profile. Other tips: A light touch of brown contour-cream between your breasts will add depth . . . blusher makes your nipples two bright spots of color that distract from your dimensions . . . white breasts against a tanned brown body look larger.

Chicken Neck
Description: Your neck bones and collarbone stick out. There is a hump in the center of your chest, above your breasts. *Cure:* Wear yokes of Cleopatra neck jewelrey, or fake pearls, or an Isadora scarf. These necklaces will be erotic against your naked body . . . disguise becomes enhancement. If you have long hair, wear it down, flowing over your shoulders and across your upper chest.

Fat Stomach
Description: Tummy pouches out. *Cure:* Hold it in as long as you can remember. (That won't be long.) Wear the frailest jewelry belt (a thin gold chain . . . your navel necklace) to remind you. Even still, you may let it all hang out eventually. Lie on your back, so stomach flattens. Tanned

tummies look smaller. Warning: Don't eat a lot that day—anyone's tummy shrinks somewhat when it's *empty*. Now, start those sit-ups! (Tomorrow?)

Ripple Thighs
Description: Thighs are loose, pucker with fat bubbles. *Cure:* Be seen seated. Lift your legs higher than usual when you walk. When lying, lift knees so that thighs are not splayed out against mattress, the loose flesh will fall *sort of* invisibly beneath the thigh bone.

Flop-over Hips
Description: Hips bulge out at sides. Your hip measurement exceeds your chest measurement (36–24–42). *Cure:* Stand with one leg in front of the other, jut pelvis forward. Keep hands over bulges whenever possible. Lie down a lot.

Washboard Behind
Description: Rear end dissolves in puckered ridges. Flesh is pocked with fat deposits. *Cure: Face* him! Stay away from overhead light (which will cast shadows and accentuate the waffled look). Little night-lights plugged into floor-level sockets are no better—they cast the light *upward,* reverse the shadows. You need *flat* light. If he wants to see your fanny (he imagines it's *cute*), roll over while lying down. Gravity will work with you while you're on your stomach; buttocks will appear round and smooth in this pose. Don't try to tighten and clench derrière muscles—puckers pull in and look *deeper* than ever. Keep it loose!

Scars, Stretch Marks
Description: Thickened tissue at the site of old wounds or where skin was pulled (as in pregnancy). *Cure:* Scars will whiten with age. If they're still red, use eye-lightener cream or Erace. Keep scars soft with lotion. Don't suntan or the contrast will worsen. Remember Raquel Welch's stretch marks . . . who notices *them?*

Fat All Over
Description: You are more than ten or fifteen pounds overweight. You have *rolls* of fat, are really heavy, and *should* do something about it. Meanwhile —*Cure:* Don't sit around nude. In *that* pose the rolls of fat tumble over one another and you look like a female Buddha. Lie or stand, and always *stretch* for as long a line as possible. Move slowly or you'll jiggle. Diet tomorrow—and keep at it!

Skinny All Over
Description: You're ten or more pounds *under*weight. Your bones are

barely upholstered. (You probably look *sensational* in clothes!) *Cure:* Extra lotions to make you *feel* softer than you look. Try to relax, move fluidly, so you don't seem even more angular. Bend over so your tiny breasts fall forward, look larger. *You* need never fear being viewed from the rear. In fact, you can even leap and dance—no flab to wobble. Play the gazelle. And have a few chocolates. It could be much worse.

If you're self-conscious about any of these naked truths, do read and absorb the suggestions as soon as possible, instead of waiting for the night before *The Night*. Flattering ways to move, sit, stand, lie down, should become *natural* to you, so you follow them unthinkingly. Boning up on techniques at the last minute will only heighten your self-consciousness. ("Oh my God, I'm standing and I'm supposed to be lying down so my tummy flattens" . . . "Eeek, he just caught a glimpse of me in profile!") Remember above all: *Nothing* should interfere in any way with the moment-to-moment pleasure of being with a man you're fond of. If there comes a time when you have to choose between backing against a wall to conceal a flawed derrière and fetching your lover his favorite lemon fizz from the kitchen, I *do* hope you'll know your priorities!

The Sensual Nude: Erotic Ideas
- thin gold chain dangling over your bare, browned skin
- painted toenails—vermilion, gold, silver?
- pretend tattoo (painted on)—small, temporary, on one breast or buttock
- waist-long hair
- beauty mark—anywhere unexpected
- perfumed powder on your fanny
- jewel in your navel (use spirit gum)
- feather fan to wave over your breasts, over his genitals
- ribbons hanging from your hair
- shoulder-length filigree earrings
- satin pillow—beside your hips
- thick brass slave bracelet on one bare upper arm
- antique watch on a chain—ticking between your breasts
- musky perfume near your secret hollows
- bizarre peacock eye makeup
- long ivory cigarette holder between your lips
- elbow-length kid gloves
- african amulet around your neck
- body painting on your stomach
- velvet choker

Bedtime Preparations

You *do* want to be able to float hand-in-hand toward the bedroom at *any* moment . . . but to insure maximum spontaneous pleasure once you *get* there, remember these *very* few beforehand details:

- Go to the bathroom before going to the bedroom—a full bladder can be very uncomfortable under the pressures of sex. If you've found from previous experience that a *slightly* full bladder heightens your sexual sensitivity (many people *do* feel that way), you may skip this visit—as long as you haven't had seven beers!
- If you think you may need extra lubrication (and first night "nerves" may dry you out), put a little sterile jelly like KY into your vagina before joining your lover.
- Take a drink if you feel that would relax you—but don't relax *too* much. Anticipatory tension adds to the excitement. You don't want to relax to the limp-rag-doll point!
- Make sure your contraceptive is in effect: We assume if you're on the Pill, you've taken it. Diaphragm can be inserted within two hours before sex, so no need to pry out of an embrace to run to the bathroom. If things progress more slowly than planned, you may need an extra dab of contraceptive jelly. Keep a supply under your bed or in a drawer you can reach *without* leaving the bed.

Love Motions in Bed

Naked you and your man are now in bed. We hope much of what you read in this chapter will just flow automatically, natural and right—as if you'd *always* known it—when you're with your man. Don't struggle to remember chapter and verse ("Let's see, am I supposed to stroke his tummy now, or does that come later?"); just do whatever comes to mind, whatever you and he *want* to do. If you've read all the *previous* chapters in this book—and followed the advice—much of your sexual know-how should be *instinctive* by now, nerve endings acutely receptive. You have no inhibitions. You know what you like . . . and you like the man.

*N*obody can say when sexual activity actually *starts*. Yes, in the Masters and Johnson labs a scientist can chart the beginnings of sexual *response*— but you're not in a lab, you're in a private place with one man you like. Perhaps just the sight of him arouses you . . . or you begin to touch each other long before the thought of bed is even a conscious one. Those preliminary longings and caresses are part of the sexual experience you're *already* sharing.

Light touches build up sexual pleasure and tension. You can indicate the way *you* like to be touched by doing the same to *him*. If you like gentle fluttery strokes, flutter away across his chest or legs. If you like to be firmly massaged, ask him—or *show* him!

Erotic Suggestions
- Touch your man lightly everywhere but his genitals—let your hand wave over them with tantalizing promise.
- Move your lover's hand to your breast, let him feel your nipples stiffen.
- Bend over him, let your long hair or hanging breasts caress him gently . . . all over his body.
- Start light. Touch gently, and move away, then back. After all, the whole idea is to *prolong* each delicious pleasure-sensation to its utmost! You have *time!*

Unarousing Things Not to Do
- *Don't give orders.* ("Touch my breasts!") Let your hands guide his until you learn how sensitive he is. Breathy instructions can be whispered later on.
- *Don't avoid looking at his penis.* Remember how touchy men are about their penises. If you don't look and *admire,* your man may feel rejected. Do say or show him you *love* his marvelous penis!
- *Don't criticize his physique.* Overlook his flaws. You will hurt him if you say "What a paunch!" or "Ugh, that hair on your back."

Gradually the tempo and pressure of your touches will increase—as you both *want* them to. You can stroke his back and buttocks more heavily, give light but direct caresses to his penis and scrotum. Remember that the under side and tip of his penis are most sensitive! If you seize him too firmly, especially at first, he may recoil. Gently pat it "better," or plant a butterfly kiss. Many men prefer to have their penises stimulated vigorously; *Ask* him what he likes—no harder than whispering, "Tell me what you like." Tell him—or show him—what *you* like. You can encourage him to caress your clitoral area and vaginal lips by putting his hand there, moaning softly—the sounds you want to make will arouse him *more,* so don't be timid. If his fingers are awkward, guide them with your own.

Kissing each other's bodies is friendly and exciting. Masters and Johnson lament the widespread belief that only a *woman's* sexual responsiveness occurs all over her body while a man's is centered on his genitals. *Not so,* they say: Freely expressive men can feel sensual pleasure *everywhere*, just like you. He will probably *adore* the sensations of your lips and tongue as you kiss his tummy, his nipples, his toes, the small of his back. He will reciprocate!

Genital kisses are lovely, too. (In fact, large numbers of people prefer this form of lovemaking to all the rest and bring each other to orgasm that way. You will find out what *you two* enjoy best as you get to know each other intimately on this night and all the ones to follow.)

Taking his penis into your mouth is called *fellatio*. If you enjoy the pleasures of this most intimate way to make love, you will just naturally find the techniques that will delight you and your man the most: quick, fluttering kisses along the length of his penis shaft, a slow, gentle kiss enclosing the tip, or long, deep kisses that draw the entire length of his penis back and forth, in and *almost* out of your mouth. Flick your tongue over the tip, around the sides, along the little cleft in the head. You can be as gentle or as forceful as he likes, but don't bite down or let your teeth scrape him. Also, *do* be cautioned that the word "sucking" is a *misnomer* for friction—we have never heard of a man who actually liked to have his penis *sucked* for more than a moment or two: The vacuumlike effect causes congestion of blood and is apt to be rather painful! (Many men *do* like that sensation at the moment of ejaculation.)

Surely he will want to give *you* silky tongue-caresses, too. When *he* stimulates *your* genital area with his mouth, the whole delightful process is called *cunnilingus*. Most men *enjoy* it! Women find it ecstatic.

Perhaps you and your man will prefer *simultaneous* oral-genital embrace, where each partner kisses the other at the same time. Or maybe you will want to stimulate each other in turns. Some couples find that mutual contact heightens each partner's excitement; others find it hard to *concentrate* on pleasing and being pleased at the same time. You will find whatever makes you feel *really* passionate will work the best.

Most men *love* oral-genital sex, but if you should find yourself in bed with one who *doesn't*, you won't *force* him! Your man may be inhibited, shy, or just prefer other contacts. (If you *want* him to share this pleasure with you, read Chapter Eleven on "How to Make Him a Better Lover," where you'll learn more about his feelings and how to deal with them.)

His penis has entered you. *Ah*. Relax, enjoy this intimate connection with your man. By now your sensuality apparatus, so carefully tuned, has gone into effect. Every thrust, every roll, every rocking motion . . . all will send shivers of delight through you. You shouldn't have to cold-bloodedly *plan* Position Sixteen. *Forget* the manuals and diagrams ("The man lies astride the woman, his thighs between her flanks, *blah blah.*") Technicalities are for people who *can't* respond! Your body and his will take over, moving you both from one position to another. Feel *free!* If the impulse is there to flip over and sit on his tummy . . . do it! If he twists you around so your back fits spoonlike against his belly while his penis works in and out . . . so be it! *Flow* with the current of sex. Any position that feels good, doesn't hurt, is wonderful.

Just because his penis is inside you doesn't mean the *rest* of your bodies have become *desensitized!* Don't stop caressing each other . . . stroke, pat, or lightly pinch whatever part of him is available.

Sex Strokes
- Your hands caress his back while he lies on top.
- You feel his tiny nipples while he sits astride you.
- You reach under and cup his scrotum as he rocks over you.
- Tenderly, you reach up and touch his cheek.
- Possessively, you hold the root of his penis while it plunges to and fro.
- You rest both palms on his shoulders and knead them.
- While you sit on top, you press your palms against his belly.
- You hold his penis and guide it inside you.
- You part, breathless, kiss each other's genitals, then begin all over again.

All the while, your man will be caressing your breasts, face, back, buttocks. You can whisper, "Oh, I like that," "There, *there*," "Squeeze me tighter," "Lift me up."

Savor the sex. No hurry. You can have the next hour . . . the whole dark night . . . an infinity of joining flesh-to-flesh. A prostitute can perform the entire sex "act" in less than fifteen minutes. If it's only an act, that's about all the time it's *worth.* For *you,* sex is not an "act," a unit with a rigidly defined start and finish and specified duties in between—it's getting into bed with a man you like, finding ways to please each other. Who can say exactly when it "started"? When it will be "over"? Who has the right to tell you what *must* go on during sex? So remember, there's no need to hurry mechanically along as though fulfilling Masters and Johnson's Four Stages of Sexual Response is your Final Exam. Forget the research findings, the rules, the "objectives" of orgasm and ejaculation, the standards set up by movies and novels, the *time* . . . think only of this man, his body and yours, and how lovely it is to be together . . . lovely enough to stretch out for as long as you want.

*W*hat if *he* rushes through in four minutes and thinks it's "over," like a short-playing record? Don't panic . . . and *don't* give in to his notion that *that* is sex. Perhaps the stimuli of a first night with a new woman have overwhelmed him. Be understanding . . . but show him that *you* don't think the evening has ground to a definite halt—otherwise he might get up and start putting on his pants. Hug and kiss him. (Don't start massaging his penis—it's probably quite sensitive right after ejaculation, and most men don't like having it touched then in any but the lightest way. Also, he may think you are demanding an instant replay.) If you have not reached orgasm, he may want to stimulate *you* with his hand or mouth until you *do*. If this pleases you, *let* him. (Some men feel *failed* otherwise.) If he doesn't mention it and *you* don't *mind*, just cuddle and touch . . . you will arouse each other over and over. Your goal with this man is to let him know that you enjoy being with him in bed, that you have lots of time, and that much erotic adventure lies *ahead*.

What if your man is impotent? He may just be extremely tense. Modern men face an awesome task: Woman's orgasm unfortunately exerts an almost tyrannical role in our society, and he may feel duty-bound to get you there the first time out. He may be self-conscious about his body, or worried about his technique. (Yes, despite the lingering vestiges of the "double standard," men *do* have the same fears as women—perhaps *more* of them, since they have traditionally borne the pressure to "perform," and their "performance" is more *verifiable* than yours. You, of course, are helping to change all those antiquated standards, because you enjoy taking an active role, but until the sexual millennium, fears of failure will continue to haunt many men.) Help dissolve the pressure. Take a breather. Play checkers. Lie in bed listening to music. Watch a funny old movie on TV. Take a wine-and-cheese break. Assure him there's no hurry. Nine cases out of ten will come through before the hero dispatches the villain or the wine bottle is empty. (The true impotent? Well, he may have serious problems—we'll tell you more about him in Chapter Eleven.)

*R*ight now, let's get back to the man who *can* enjoy his—and *your*— sexuality to the fullest.

Sex is a delicious state that you'll be in as long as you're together, even while you're not *actually* making love. You'll glide into a feeling of warmth and contentment, lie close and still, murmur endearments, give each other sleepy hugs and "thank you" kisses. You may want to shower together. Or for a quickie "cleanup" in bed, dry each other with a towel and share a light friction rub or cream massage.

How much energetic sexual activity can you expect on a first night? Since the excitement is so *new,* probably a *lot.* More if your lover has just come back from six months on all-male lighthouse guard duty or if the presex buildup was going on clandestinely for six months over the office water cooler; less if you met your man two hours ago at a singles' bar and haven't had much time to build up sexual static.

Should the man stay over or go home in the dark of night? That depends:
- Does he want to stay? (He *does* if he has set the alarm for the next morning, unpacked a razor, asked for an extra pillow, or simply announced "I want to spend the night with you.")
- Do you want him to stay? (If the experience wasn't what you had hoped for, and you don't want to face him in the bleak dawn, suggest—gently—that he depart).

If you've had the kind of super sex we think you'll have, your man may naturally stay over—he'll be too exhausted to move, too anxious to see you over breakfast.

Final thoughts before we say goodnight: As you are drawn closer together by sex, the man who entered your bed as a virtual stranger becomes a lover. You share a thousand secrets of the flesh, all delicious. No matter what happens next, you *know* one another. You have *shared.* Communicated. Whether you someday part or not, that essential link will always remain between you. One woman we know was startled to see a man on an airplane ten years after she'd last made love with him: "A whole *flood* of sensations overwhelmed me when I looked into his eyes. Instantly, I remembered his weight on my body, the special intense way he had of melting against me . . . pressing hard but gently. He used to bury his face in my hair and whisper my name. He recognized me on the plane at once. We exchanged only pleasantries (my new husband was with me), but our looks were very knowing. I felt warm and flushed during the whole flight. I still think of him."

Somebody has said, "Once lovers, always lovers." And in a sense that is true. You and your man will always remember the pleasure you shared no matter what happens afterward. That's why many lovers stay friends, and help each other out with tax returns, apartments, advice, dinner invitations. No matter how long it lasted, it's a relationship. Ah, love!

Ways
to sustain
lust

$\mathcal{L}$ust—that devilish look in his eye . . . the quickening of your heartbeat . . . a deep-sinking warmth between your legs.

It thrives on first nights. Suspense makes it *easy:* "Will he or won't he?" . . . "What will it be like with him?" . . . "What will we do tonight?" Exploration keeps your pulse—and his—pounding. When that first night stretches to a second, then a third, then, finally, into an infinity of nights in the long affair (or marriage), lust may go limp.

Long-term sexual relationships demand imagination and energy. Your bodies can no longer supply the surprises that lit the *first* spark. So you have to be terribly clever, invent ways to keep passion alive.

First, assess the damage. Your sex relations with one man have been going on for some months or years. (We don't expect ennui to set in within *weeks.*) Chart your sex quotient and see if passion is on the wane.

High ratings if:
- You make love every night you're together.
- You have orgasms often.
- He wakes you from sleep for love in the middle of the night—and loves it when *you* wake *him.*
- He arrives at unexpected hours to seize you and throw you to the bed.

Falling ratings if:
- You make love dutifully, quickly, and not as often as you used to when you first became lovers.

- One or both of you can watch television while making love.
- You've settled into one position.
- He no longer exclaims over your perfect breasts, the way you wriggle your hips, how you stroke him.
- You occasionally say, "I'm too tired. In the morning, maybe."

Low ratings if:
- You offered him a choice of a ham sandwich or you, and he picked the ham sandwich.
- He used your nightie to polish his shoes.
- His head swivels every time another woman passes.
- He's stopped wearing his elevator shoes with you.
- You make love once a week.
- He asks what you're doing when you try something unexpected in bed.

Danger ratings if:
- You make love once a year—on your birthday.
- You make love once a year—on his *mother's* birthday.
- He's suggested you meet other men.
- One or both of you fall asleep in front of the television every night.
- He's hanging up *Playboy* centerfolds again.
- You fall asleep during sex.

If your man is making love to you at least once a night, flipping you into different creative positions each time . . . and you are responding with endless quivers of ecstasy, read no more. You don't need this chapter. *But* if you've noticed any of the depreciation listed in the lower ratings, plow ahead. It's not too late to rekindle lust!

Don't give up on a sexual relationship you still want unless (1) the man has gone, (2) he doesn't speak to you, or (3) he's paralyzed from the waist down. Lust can be revived in all other cases—if you try, and if you *really* desire him. Even in the dire instance of the man who makes love to you only once a year—on your birthday—hope flickers: He still remembers your birthday! Bring back the zest. Break the following:

Bad Sex Habits
- You *always* make love after the late evening news.
- He's on top of you at a 45° angle—every night.

- Sex happens in bed—never anywhere else.
- Your amours last fifteen minutes per session.
- You've worn the same nightie for thirty nights in a row.
- A shower afterward is *de rigeur.*
- You both repeat the same tired phrases each time: "You're driving me wild, Baby" . . . "I'm so hot I could die."
- After making love, you trot straight to the bathroom to douche.
- Your lovemaking follows a rigid pattern: five minutes of kissing, two minutes of caressing, then *Bang!*
- You've started to complain about him to your friends.

As soon as a sex practice becomes a habit, the thrill fades. Try to vary sexual behavior. Instead of flopping into that bedtime routine, make love while you still have maximum energy. Many men *ache* with desire during the day . . . many women love making love before breakfast. Be available for a noontime rendezvous. *Special precautions:* Daylight can be a bit *stark.* Draw blinds. Also, if you have to dart back to an office, be sure to leave time to freshen up: You don't want to undulate in, wafting the aromas of love.

*T*he ideal time for extended sex bouts is the weekend—plenty of free time and energy for both of you. Instead of capitalizing on these love-hours, too many people turn the weekends into work marathons—drive to car washes, rent U-Hauls, clip grass, shop, sew clothes, do enormous loads of laundry. Okay, you have to tend to chores *sometime,* but try to save huge chunks of every *other* weekend or at least Sunday for pure, un-interrupted lovemaking. *Special precautions:* Take time to rest together, eat hearty fare—or he may conk out and read the Sunday funnies.

Morning sex can be great. Many men awake erect anyway (although this condition should not be interpreted as an indisputable sign of uncon-trollable lust for you. Latest medical research shows that regular morning erection has nothing to do with sexual desire—it's just the way a man's body responds to a certain phase of the dream cycles we all have. Of course, if you're there beside him, he may want to make pleasant use of the phenomenon!) *Special precautions:* Use a breath mint (morning bad breath is no aphrodisiac); keep mints hidden in bedside table, or leave a glass of water there the night before. Also, take care that the alarm clock won't go off during lovemaking. Alarm clocks are rotten for the nerves at *any* time. During sex, an alarm can shatter the circuits and leave you both atremble and irritable all day. Be sure to allow plenty of time: He will fondly recall the lovemaking all day—if it hasn't made him late for work. One last warning: Don't go back to sleep!

Is there any reason why you *must* make love in a *bed?* Leap in and surprise your man in the shower. Warm, wet, wriggling—you'll be irresistible. The steady beat of the shower and the new sensation of wet skin against wet skin will feel excitingly new. *Special precautions:* Install a rubber non-slip mat on tub or shower-stall floor, or you may end up in a full body cast. Watch out for falling bars of soap, sponges, bath brushes. Suggested: If you look rotten with your hair wet, try bathtub sex instead. Draw a bubble bath, jump in, and call him to "wash your back."

Outdoor sex? The natural surroundings should be wildly exciting. Your senses can be stimulated by the scents of grass, newly mown hay, pine needles, the chirping of crickets, whatever happens to be around. In the movie *Women in Love,* there is a fantastic sex scene in a field of flowers. Take your man out to the country or to the shore (city parks are too public), find a secluded spot. *Special precautions:* Watch out for poison ivy, poison oak, mosquitoes, wasps, poisonous snakes. Wear a bug repellent in a light spray form. (The oily versions might make sex too sticky.) Fall and spring are good seasons for outdoor sex—fewer interested spectators, cool breezes for hot bodies. Winter sex-sports are mostly for adventurers— but perhaps a sauna followed by a brisk roll in a snowbank? Encouraging note: The penis is the last part of a man's exposed body to freeze!

Auto sex (no, that's *not* self-stimulation) may have started the sexual revolution. Certainly, the backseat of a car has long been a trysting place for teen-agers. Grown-ups who finally have a *bed* somewhere can be titillated by recapturing that furtive, frustrating sex-in-a-car. *Special precautions:* Park in a private spot. Don't attempt relations in a two-seater —even Volkswagens can be a tight squeeze. Sedans suit the purpose nicely. You can be doubly naughty and love-in at a drive-in. Oh, you kid!

Not *all* lust-killers and lust-enhancers are specifically sexual. A famous James Thurber cartoon shows a vaguely frumpy-looking man saying to a vaguely frowzy-looking woman, "When did the magic go out of our marriage?" *Any* long-term relationship can be sabotaged by a thousand inadvertent turnoffs, or kindled afresh by a thousand sparks. You *know* what charms you and bugs you about your man. (Find tactful ways to *tell* him, like praising him when he does something you *like*.) Here are some common *male* likes and dislikes:

Turn-Ons

- "A bare midriff . . . That, to me, is the most provocative thing a girl can show. I love to see girls in those pajama outfits that make them look like belly dancers; bare middles are sexier than a totally bare girl, and I love to put an arm around her and suddenly feel naked flesh. Bare backs are great, too."

- "A girl who laughs from her belly button! . . . A rich, full, generous laugh means she's a rich, full, and generous woman. From my experience, girls who laugh with all of themselves love with all of themselves, too."

- "Tons of clean, shiny hair . . . I love the look of it and the smell of it, the promise of burying my face in it, feeling it caress my body. It's truly woman's crowning glory."

- "A little less than perfect . . . Hair should be a tiny bit mussed. That makes a girl look passionate and a little available. Perfect hair says 'touch me not.'"

- "Flowery smells . . . Man! those soapy, perfumy, powdery smells, they are *just* great."

- "Girls in men's clothes . . . Now that isn't as weird as it sounds. I love to see a girl lost in my sweater on the beach, or looking fragile wrapped in my bathrobe."

- "Long, long looks . . . She looks straight in my eye. Dead-level straight and she keeps looking at me sometimes. I take it as a great compliment that she's got nothing better to do or no place better to look."

- "What to wear . . . I like a girl to ask me to help her decide what to put on. Not *all* the time. But it does make you feel they're dressing just for you."

- "The shy pornographer . . . the girl who understands the nature of male arousal. There was this sweet, gentle little thing who would pull the most incredibly obscene things in a very quiet low-key way. I never knew what to expect. Like, she'd be serving us dinner at home and she'd be wearing slacks and a sweater or something, and all of a sudden I'd realize that during one trip to the kitchen she had taken off her bra, because there she'd be sitting across from me, the outlines of her bare breasts pushing through the soft sweater."

- "Peaceful, silent times . . . These can be the slowest, most exquisite of turn-ons. Mostly it depends on the girl keeping her mouth shut. Chattering ruins the mood. What I'm talking about are the quiet times of reading and listening to records or of driving or picnicking alone, when the two of you slowly respond to each other. You don't rush it. You just let it gradually happen until the suspense becomes intolerable."

- "Love at lunchtime . . . I used to date this super girl (she married someone else), and she had an apartment near my office. We once decided to have lunch at her place. I arrived, kissed her, we looked at each other, and without saying another word went to bed. We never did have lunch, just time for milk and some cookies; it was great."
- "A little experimental in bed . . . She ought to be willing to try *anything* once."
- "A private world . . . secret words and looks, a pat on the fanny that no one at the party sees. The intimate little world she makes for me."
- "Mornings with her . . . when she wakes up rosy and glowing with all that sleep. Hell, I know what women look like without their makeup and it doesn't frighten me to see she has blemishes. If she's awake and rested, she's ready to be made love to again."
- "Breasts . . . my girl *likes* to have her breasts caressed. I'm sure of it. She's the first woman I ever met who really did."
- "She's got the smoothest, creamiest behind . . . I don't know what she does, maybe she puts baby oil on it or something, but it's sensational. . . ."
- "A rounded tummy . . . a little belly that sticks out just a little bit . . . feminine and fabulous."
- "Quarts of perfume . . . all over her . . . sensuous as hell."
- "A girl who likes food . . . and eats with gusto. Girls who have good appetites at the table are generally great in bed."
- "She puts me ahead of the dishes. . . . She lets them wait instead of her man."
- "She gets into the shower with me."
- "She respects my weaknesses. . . . I don't feel as if I'm on trial all the time."
- "She tells me what she likes in bed. . . . She's not a traffic cop but she lets me know what turns *her* on and off."
- "She worries about me. . . . One rainy night, I picked her up. We were going to a party. My shoes were a mess. She made me take them off and then she polished them. I was really touched by the sight of this sweet, loving girl polishing my shoes. I felt like a million bucks."

- "She goes out of her way to excite me. . . . One night she arrived at my place in a maxicoat—with nothing on underneath."
- "Maybe I'm a voyeur of sorts . . . but I love watching a girl brushing her hair or sewing a button on or knitting something. It makes me want to take her in my arms and kiss her."
- "She knows when to be crude. . . . She whispers erotic things to me on the way home—or something during a boring dinner party. She has a great sense of timing. Sometimes I could kill her—but not really."
- "She makes a pass at me. . . . She is the aggressor, but in a loving way, not a demanding way. Some girls demand 'Make love to me!'"
- "She has a sense of priorities. . . . Say we had been planning to go to the movies but then we got comfortable at home. She's not rigid about insisting on the movies. She doesn't say, 'You promised.'"
- "She says thank you. . . . She doesn't feel 'entitled,' but appreciates things like being picked up in the rain."

Turn-Offs
- "The Horror-Scope Kid . . . The first thing she wants to know is when's your birthday. Then, she gives you an instant horoscope reading of your sign and how it's the perfect combination with her sign! Let me out!"
- "Ptomaine Mary . . . Obviously her taste buds were destroyed at birth. She thinks she can cook. She cannot cook. She insists on cooking. It's cruelty to animals. Namely, me."
- "Two-tone hair . . . O.K., so she's not really a blonde, but if she wants to be a blonde, she should be all blonde. I don't mind streaking done by a good hairdresser, but there's nothing crummier-looking than black roots. It looks like a disease."
- "Harpo Marx wigs . . . It's incredible the way some girls look like they're wearing a dirty curly floor mop on their heads—and you're supposed to think all those curls are their real hair? Who do they think they're kidding?"
- "The Correction Officer . . . I divorced two wives because each one, in turn, could not resist correcting my grammar, table manners, tastes. I realize I *picked* the wives but now I'm wary of the 'professor type.' Women who feel that

they must correct men's public habits tend to do the same in more intimate settings, too. I can't believe I was doing *everything* wrong!"

- "This obsession with New Year's Eve . . . drives me mad. You know, I leave town now rather than get into a hassle. I don't mind taking a girl out on New Year's Eve; I like those big parties. But your date regards it as some kind of a lifelong commitment. And they start leaning on you about it in October."

- "Her medical report . . . I love her body, yes, but I don't want to hear detailed reports about what the gynecologist said and did and how this affects her tubes, drainage, and other female plumbing."

- "She had this allergy . . . and she kept telling me about her rash and what certain pills did to her digestive processes, and once, when she had some fancy dental work, she kept opening her mouth and making me look at the filling and things. *Icch.*"

- "The girl who asks, 'Are you married?' . . . Those girls with the white knuckles who clutch tight at your arms as if you were a life preserver. You don't happen to be married. You're not totally opposed to the idea. But my blood congeals when I start circling in on a girl at a party and she looks at me with cold, suspicious eyes, demanding to know my marital status. It's as if she won't even risk a few minutes of small talk unless I show her my bankbooks and draft card and vow to make an honest woman of her."

- "The girl who eats garlic."

- "Dirty bra straps."

- "Hair spray that feels like shellac . . . Who wants to caress a bowling ball?"

- "The girl who tells you . . . about all the rich, handsome, brilliant men who want to marry her."

- "The girl who goes to bed with you . . . and then acts like a martyr, subjecting herself to all this dirtiness."

Some men (maybe yours!) warm up or (horrors!) freeze over at *these* habits . . . can you *guess* which are hot, which cold?

- "Hugging me and fogging my glasses."
- "Telling me she's on a diet."
- "A crocheted dress with a nude bodystocking."
- "Drinking too much and throwing up."

- "An impromptu striptease."
- "Taking me to a wedding where she catches the bouquet."
- "Reading poetry we both love. Aloud."
- "Interrupting, and that includes jokes and lovemaking."
- "I love you."
- "Let's get married."
- "I thought we'd stay home tonight."
- "My parents are coming over."
- "The private, intimate 'we'."
- "The public, possessive 'we'."
- "Weeping from sheer ecstasy."
- "Crying in order to get her own way—and getting a red nose instead."
- "A truly great lemon meringue pie in the refrigerator for a 4 A.M. raid."
- "Talking baby talk."
- "Calling me to say goodnight."
- "Calling me by the wrong name."
- "Singing ribald songs."
- "Giving naked massages."
- "Looking down at my slacks—*there.*"
- "Being found "asleep" on the couch."
- "Telling me her sex dreams."
- "Saying that she dreamed it was me, not Robert Redford after all."
- "Asking me if all men are such wonderful lovers."
- "Confessing a secret, tiny perversion . . . like wanting to make love with the lights on."
- "Whispering her favorite part of my body."
- "Touching me while I'm wearing clothes."
- "Describing how she felt the last time we made love."

Separate apartments *do* make it easier to keep the embers glowing. You'll be more independent, less clinging, and endlessly fascinating because of it! Try alternating lovemaking locales from your place to his— the change is good for your affair. Your own apartment also gives you a sense of security. (Always having the *option* to leave him—even if you never exercise it—is a tantalizing psychological plus.) It's a place to go and rethink things when you fight, a haven for rest and recuperation, a place where you *can* wander around with olive-oil conditioner on your hair and herbal mask on your face. It also gives you the chance to fit concurrent affairs into your life if you wish.

Do keep in touch with your lover even when he's out of sight. If you can write an amusing letter, send him one, even if you'll see him in a few days. A heavy-breathing style doesn't suit every man—evaluate him before you dash off purple prose. One smart girl we know sends her man telegrams, but without gushy messages. The most recent one: "I LIKE YOUR MOUSTACHE." Her lover said the telegram made him smile, want to see her, hold her . . . tickle her lips with his moustache. Avoid tacky gimmicks:

- "funny" cards from Woolworth's that say, "Why haven't you called me . . . you fink?" Your personal message *has* to be better.
- calling at midnight—drunk, or just plain slobbering
- knocking at his door uninvited
- asking your friends (or *his*) if they've seen him with another girl.

Instead, keep in touch in an attractive, dignified way. You can call a man during the day to tell him:

- You just read a book he'd like.
- You're making his favorite bouillabaisse that night.
- Something wonderful has happened to you—and you *had* to share it with him!

You'll make him *want* to see you, not feel trapped.

When he calls you, make him lust. Men are vulnerable to the sound of a dusky voice purring in their ear. Their imaginations run wild. They want more. Feed his fantasy. Provide an appealing vision of yourself. Never mind that in reality you are standing in your Dr. Scholl's orthopedic sandals and your face is cracking with dried Clearasil . . . he'll never guess. Let it slip, in deep, breathy tones, that you were just:

- in the shower. Image: You—shimmering wetly, Bardot-like in this tiny towel that barely covers your cleavage and rounded bottom. The towel is slipping as you hold the phone . . . *ooops!*
- fast asleep. Image: You—a sensuous sleepwalker, warm-skinned underneath a lacy peignoir, with sleep-heavy thighs and a voice muffled by dreams and sighs . . .
- reading the *Kama Sutra*. Image: You—in a receptive pretzel pose. He may rush right over!

If *you're* still interested in the man, you will *naturally* find a thousand new ways to tell him so—and inspire *him* to do the same for you. *Don't* feel you must rivet him at every waking moment with intricate sexual novelties and mysterious threats of other lovers . . . simply *love* him.

*How to
make him
a better lover*

ELEVEN

Most men are not good lovers. There, I've said it—and so, probably, have you. (Maybe you even thought it was *you* who were doing something "wrong," failing to respond!) Most men *do not know* how to please a receptive woman.

But, I hasten to add, it's *not* the poor darlings' *fault*. Cultural conditioning has turned the average American male into a *klutz*. After all, here *you* are reading this book: *You* want to learn to be a better lover. For a woman in our society, a "Please the men!" platform is acceptable (though I hope you're concerned with pleasing *yourself*, too!) But until recently, few American *men* were encouraged to study lovemaking to please *women*. It was enough that the male *conquered*. Sex was *his* "satisfaction," her "*duty*." "Performance" centered on *his* ability to maintain *his* erection— and had little to do with the woman's *response*. A strong "machismo" myth outlawed tenderness; men were taught to "score," not *love*.

Our heritage, the Anglo-Saxon American, is particularly at fault. (In some cultures, notably Italian and French, men have long practiced the art of love with real flair and interest in women.) *American* boy babies receive even less cuddling than the little dished out to girls. Boys are raised to *restrain* emotion, keep their hands to themselves, and not expect, or welcome, embraces from family or friends. Sense-deprived through childhood, their only sexual outlet is masturbation . . . and society has made sure they feel guilty about *that*. Then the sweaty, ashamed little graspings begin in the long fumble through adolescence. Most men you know had their first sex experience with a girl in the backseat of a car. The conditions scarcely encouraged sensual dalliance. A "hurry—get it over with" feeling took root. A man's sexual technique may not have improved much since those hasty, frantic matings.

$\mathcal{M}$eanwhile, as a girl, you suffered through a similarly schizophrenic sex training. Everything about sex was *verboten* until you became marriageable; then presto! . . . you were suddenly supposed to know how to respond to the heretofore guarded mystery. Groping adolescent boys wanted you to "put out," but what were *you* supposed to get in return? Nobody explained what *you* should expect in the way of pleasure—only what the *man* wanted and how to fulfill him. "Always pretend to have an orgasm" . . . "Tell him he's a wonderful lover so that he won't leave you for another woman." Lie! Lie! Lie!

Women's liberation and general enlightenment are undoing some of the damage now. But there are too many crummy lovers around who've been convinced they are super by girls who *lied*. Let's re-educate ourselves *and* the men. We'll both have more pleasure.

In the interim, as reassurance to all women who have suffered with incompetent lovers and blamed *themselves*, here are:

The Ten Most Common Mistakes Men Make in Bed

1. Judging by his readiness alone. Because *his* penis is erect, he assumes *you're* red-hot. Sexual readiness varies with every individual on every occasion. Don't *you* wait for *him* if the situation is reversed?
2. Quitting early. You're starting to respond, but just as you warm up, he pulls out, rolls over, and goes to sleep.
3. Routinizing requests for sex. Some men have a one-liner stock-in-trade, like the husband in *Diary of a Mad House-wife*'s "How about a little roll in de hay?" Other grim possibilities: "How about it?" "Want to . . . ?" "Can't we do it before dinner?" "We've got fifteen minutes before the Smiths get here."
4. Giving orders. Bred to assume an authoritarian role, the American male may *tell* you to perform some special act on him or move in a certain way. He makes you feel you're *servicing* him.
5. Bad timing. Every night at ten. Or worse, only every Saturday night. Or worse still, in the morning *before* he brushes his teeth.
6. Careless grooming. Speaking of teeth—how's his breath, beard, body odor? Many a girl has pampered and powdered herself only to be suffocated by unshowered, unshaved Hubby. (Lovers, of course, usually do better.)

7. Choosing unrealistic locations. The urge comes upon him strong and swift, so he seizes you in a hallway, idling car, train station, or some other place where you feel ill at ease.

8. Demanding praise. Not only is he a poor lover, but he *wants* to be told he's *fantastic*. He needs to think he's the *best* lover you've had, and constantly hounds you and demands a "yes" to the tiresome question, "Did you come?" (You didn't.)

9. Turning off afterward. The sex may have been passable, even good—but then lover rolls over like a beached whale. You murmur, "I love you." He groans, snores, or snuffles into the pillow. Few men stick around to hug and kiss when you would like it most.

10. Being too smooth. Everything progresses so professionally: ten minutes to your breasts, five minutes for heavy petting, four minutes of oral contacts . . . you feel *programmed* . . . sense he uses the same systematic technique on *every* girl. He may satisfy your body—not your soul.

$\mathcal{P}$oor lovers abound, and may commit not one but several of the most common mistakes mentioned. The men who err fall into several types— some are inexperienced but well-meaning (I think these are the majority), others are selfish or boorish. Here are some common categories:

- *Minuteman.* He's a premature ejaculator. It's all over in seconds. He may be too fast because he's overly excited, very young and inexperienced, nervous about you, or a just plain poor lover who regards sex as a function, such as going to the bathroom. The young, nervous fellow is worth your time. The one with the peculiar ideas needs psychotherapy.

- *Stanley Kowalski.* A common species who will make love before a blaring TV, blast beer (or martini) breath in your face, hurl the full weight of his 250 pounds upon you, and possibly belch afterward.

- *King Kong.* Thinks all women want to be pushed around, doesn't stop thrusting when a girl cries "Ouch!" and *means* it. A rough character who may really hate women.

- *Charlie Brown.* A cute, little-boy lover who wants to be tickled and babied, offers nothing in return. He may spend a lot of time "nursing" around your nipples. Some girls find Charlie endearing. Most women like grown-ups.

- *Invisible Man.* Now you see his erection, now you don't. If he isn't terribly old, sick, or drunk, he needs professional therapy.
- *Shylock.* He bargains for sex, *expects* it after an expensive evening, even barters in bed: "I'll do this to you . . . *if* you'll do that to me." Maybe even, "I'll come now. I'll let you the next time around." Some girls don't mind Shylock —if they think it's a fair trade. Others find the "pound of flesh" too dear.
- *Hamlet.* This indecisive lover over-emotes through inter-course, may weep, shriek, scream, beg. He could be dis-concerting to a girl looking for more casual pleasure.
- *Drill Instructor.* Gives snappy commands: "Turn over! Lie down! Sit up!" He'll put you through your paces until you wish you'd never enlisted.
- *Athlete.* He performs in bed as if he were on a trampoline. His dexterity and good physique would be welcome if he wasn't quite so *sporty* and didn't cry "Wheee!" and "Upsy-daisy!" at crucial points.
- *Robot.* He's *technically* perfect—all gears and cogs in working order. But do you get the feeling he's reading a manual over your shoulder?
- *Professor Higgins.* He insists on teaching you his technique: "No, not that way! Don't thrust your pelvis like that . . . " and so on until you transfer out of his class. Of course, a little instruction may be in order, but no man should be critical or pedantic in bed!
- *Dr. Masters.* He's a self-styled liberator, up on *all* the latest research about female sexual response. See his deftness as he massages your clitoris for hours with one index finger; even though you say you can't *bear* the sensation any more, he knows *better.* Pretty soon you feel like you're on a stain-less-steel examining table in the St. Louis labs—which is maybe where this lover belongs.
- *Sir Galahad.* His quest isn't the Holy Grail—it's the Female Orgasm. He will labor over you for hours, won't *ever* give up—even if you have the flu or are exhausted from playing six sets of tennis at Wimbledon. He *means* awfully well, but pretty soon you get to thinking that a man hell-bent on giving you an orgasm under *any* circumstances is just about the most boring person alive. Who is he trying to please, anyway—you or his ego?
- *Oblomov:* Like the sleepy hero of the Russian novel,

Oblomov is too *lazy* to make good love. He may be stoned on drugs, drunk, or just an inert guy. He makes *you* do all the action. Fortunately, Oblomovs are rare, and seldom have the energy to go out and meet you.

- *Fetishist*. He focuses with lurid concentration on your breasts, legs, buttocks, or earlobes, to the exclusion of the *rest*. Woman cannot live by one erogenous zone alone . . . look for more versatility.
- *Straightman*. He makes love in Position One, has no imagination, balks if you move by so much as a 5-degree angle. Change position by a 180-degree angle—walk out!
- *Mr. Apocalypse*. Maybe from reading Norman Mailer or Wilhelm Reich, he has this idea that he's missing out on the Ultimate Orgasm just beyond his grasp. He is never satisfied that sex with a mortal woman has been the Profound Psychic Experience it *could* be. He may have a lot of funny ideas about energy waves. He may *also* think sex in any form but man-on-top is loathesomely *mortal*. Tell him to peddle his philosophy elsewhere.

Don't be depressed because so *many* men are poor lovers. There are also many *wonderful* lovers available—more now than *ever*, because of the upswing in healthy sexuality.

How to Tell the Men From the Boys

Cheerful signs if he:
- brings you one flower he picked himself.
- touches you while you talk to each other.
- moves his body to music.
- plays an instrument, sings, or dances a lot.
- cooks you dinner.
- wears East Indian shirts at home.
- tucks your hand in his pocket to keep it warm on an icy day.
- looks right into your eyes.
- asks if you're thirsty, and when you say "yes," brings you a glass of ice water from the kitchen.
- laughs easily.
- asks what you're thinking about.
- loves animals.

Danger if he:
- asks for soda with your *coq au vin* dinner.
- starches his T-shirts.

- chews gum incessantly.
- chews tobacco.
- spits on the street.
- beats a punching bag for hours on end.
- carries a small riding crop.
- wears a beer-can opener around his neck.
- can't help you across the street without dislocating a shoulder (yours).
- carries French postcards and rubber condoms everywhere.
- asks you to marry him on the first date.
- wants to know if you're a virgin.
- mentions his mother more than twice in an evening.

Now, many very *nice* men are poor lovers. A man can be handsome, generous, charming, intelligent, affectionate, and still have sex problems. If *your* man is one of these almost-perfect lovers, if *you* love *him*, you'll want to *help*. The effort can be *worthwhile*—and it's *easier* to get a dear man to do better at sex than reform a nasty-but-skilled Don Juan. Take your poor darling into your arms, treat him tenderly, show him you understand—and can *help*.

A surprising number of men are becoming increasingly plagued by the same fears that have traditionally hung up women . . . and, ironically, these fears may be caused in some cases by the *same* innovations—both medical and social—which today are *freeing women* from their inhibitions: the Pill, as well as changes (for the better) about what is considered accepted moral behavior in our now permissive society.

The point is that as more and more women succeed in shedding their sexual bonds and begin to make greater sexual demands on their men, the men may grow progressively more inhibited if they're not always able to meet those demands. As social anthropologist Lionel Tiger was quoted on this very subject in *Time* magazine last year: "There's something that [women] are going to have to cope with—that males are much more fragile sexually. It's often difficult for males to perform sexually if they don't feel that the mood is just right." And I don't think Tiger was speaking of isolated situations but rather the chronic sexual problems of many males.

Well, what kind of problems *do* men have when they take a woman to bed? One, of course, is that some men don't know how to get a girl there in the first place. Even in this time of relaxing cultural mores, there *are* men too inhibited or shy or awkward to make the right approaches that will lead to a night of lovemaking. They wait and hope for the *woman* to make the advances. Now certainly girls no longer *have* to play the same coy games they formerly did, but many still *expect* the male to outwardly do the chasing . . . still *feel* that the double standard requires them to "be available" rather than initiate the contact. And so, despite our new morality, most *social* intercourse between males and females today continues to look suspiciously like an old-fashioned date, even if candlelight and wine have been replaced by rock music and pot. The subtle buildup, it seems, has *yet* to give way to the direct sexual approach!

O.K., you may say, so the primary reason some women come on indirectly is because they still adhere to the double standard—but why are so many men also slaves to subtlety? *Fear of rejection.* Even in 1971 a man may be afraid to ask a girl directly for a date or to kiss her or initiate more suggestive sexual advances (what used to be called "making a pass") for fear of being rebuffed and humiliated. Of course, a man who's experienced and aware usually knows when the time for romance is right, because he's picked up on the mood of the evening, the look in a girl's eyes, closeness expressed in various ways. But some men just aren't attuned to these "yes" signs, and they're scared to death to venture even a kiss.

Now at this point you may be thinking, Wait a minute! Do I really *want* to be more intimate with this guy, however interesting or witty or handsome, if he's so unempathetic, so cowardly? If it's such a problem merely getting to kiss this man, won't anything further be out of the question? Maybe so, although a surprising number of men who eventually prove virile, warm, giving lovers have found the first kiss—because it might meet with rejection—their most difficult hurdle. Fortunately, that kind of insecurity is usually experienced only initially during any given relationship, and once it is overcome, simply vanishes.

*W*hat would you guess is the most *common* sexual insecurity men have? Believe it or not, the fear that their penises are not large enough. (Just as some women are concerned about the size of their breasts.) One man expressed his "problem" this way: "For years now I've been embarrassed and afraid of being laughed at in locker rooms, swimming pools, bathrooms, etc., because of the size of my penis. After intercourse, where I usually muster a barely adequate six inches, my penis shrinks down to one inch. One inch!" (His use of the word "muster" is quite interesting. Many men look upon sexual activity as a kind of contest, and fear they won't measure up.)

This man simply didn't *know* that his dimensions were O.K. Ours has been such a sexually repressed society until recently that many of us simply lack a sound knowledge of our own anatomy. Hard as it is to believe today, some men have had such overly protected upbringings they may never have *seen* another man in the nude . . . or certainly not with the penis in an erect state. And so they have come to rely on hearsay and exaggeration about what is deemed to be "normal." If their sex education had been more intelligent in childhood, they might be a little less anxious about themselves today.

What, then, can a woman do to *assure* her partner that he is more than adequately endowed? Well, just as you appreciate compliments about your own physical attributes, so does he. You can do no harm, even if this part of his body doesn't worry him, by saying things like, "Oh, you're really a *man*" or "You feel so good." Tell him what you *feel*.

Now let's turn to the male insecurities stemming from some very *real* problems that can afflict men both physically and emotionally:

Premature Ejaculation: This is the condition in which the male climax occurs as a man tries to initiate intercourse or a few seconds afterward. Although Dr. Alfred Kinsey, first of the sex statisticians, didn't consider P.E. a problem at all, noting that chimpanzees and other primates ejaculate within twenty seconds or so of the onset of coition, most men and their women are frustrated by this kind of "monkey" business. Masters and Johnson, whose view of the situation is more humane than Kinsey's, consider a man does indeed have a problem "if he cannot control his ejaculatory process for a sufficient length of time during intravaginal containment to satisfy his partner in at least 50 percent of their coital connections." (That is, assuming the *female* has no great orgasmic trouble.)

Premature ejaculation is common in *young* men but can also occur in any male who has been celibate for a long time or when sexual foreplay is unusually protracted. (However, extensive foreplay can be *therapeutic* for the same condition in some circumstances.) The problem is often prevalent among men who had their earliest sexual experiences with prostitutes, those disciples of the "quickie." Other males vulnerable to the problem are those who, as teen-agers, either petted to climax or got used to making love in automobiles or other confined, semipublic quarters not conducive to prolonged sexual episodes.

Several methods are used to treat premature ejaculation, depending on the individual and the severity of his problem. Usually,'when the male becomes more familiar with his sexual partner, the malfunction disappears. *Increased* sexual activity during a limited period also "cures" premature ejaculation in many men, so that while it may occur during the initial attempt of the evening, it may not again if sexual activity takes place shortly afterward. If a man engages in intercourse three times within an evening, say, it will take him longer to reach orgasm each time.

Some sexologists deal with the problem by suggesting that the man use fantasies which turn him *off*—thinking of his least favorite politician, his last hospital visit or school-cafeteria meal, or even counting sheep (ugly sheep!) Pinching the skin of the arm, flexing the toes to the point of painful spasm or cramp, biting one's tongue or the inside of the cheek, squinting the muscles around the eyes tightly—all have been known to prevent premature ejaculation.

Certain drugs known to inhibit orgasm—specifically, tranquilizers, amphetamines, sedatives—may also be prescribed to alleviate the problem. (Of course, they must be administered by a physician and used only under his supervision.) Another method that has given some men the staying power to bring a partner to orgasm is to rub anesthetic ointment into the head of the penis half an hour or so before intercourse, thereby dulling sensation in the male and lessening his chances of climaxing too *soon*.

The above measures, unfortunately, though they produce varying degrees of success, are merely expedients and not "cures." But thanks to Masters and Johnson, we now have a technique for treating premature ejaculation that is so effective (the failure rate among 186 men was only 2.2 percent) they feel the problem "can be and should be brought fully under control during the next decade"—assuming, of course, that enough physicians can be adequately trained to handle the traffic. Central to the M&J method is the "squeeze" routine, which, in essence, works this way: The female, after stimulating her partner to erection, places three fingers around the head of the penis and squeezes for three or four seconds with a pressure sufficient to make his desire to climax disappear. Actually, the process is more complicated than that—Masters and Johnson oversee two weeks of intensive therapy for every couple they treat; so for those of you with a man who has the P.E. problem, buy M&J's *Human Sexual Response* and *Human Sexual Inadequacy,* and use the books in consultation with your own physician or a qualified marriage counselor. With *proper* instruction, premature ejaculation can be overcome in nearly every male who suffers it.

Ejaculatory Incompetence: Now we come to a condition that is the direct opposite of premature ejaculation. A man who climaxes a few moments after penetration has a problem all right, but the man who begins intercourse yet cannot reach orgasm, no matter how hard he tries, is in even *worse* shape. For a woman this state of affairs may at first appear blissful—having her lover aroused for what seems like infinity. But as time passes they may both become quite irritated, literally *and* figuratively.

Two types of ejaculatory incompetence have been defined by Masters and Johnson: (1) primary—characteristic of males who cannot climax at all, though they can maintain an erection (the incidence is rare and the cause almost surely physical); (2) secondary—seen in males who cannot reach orgasm during lovemaking but can through masturbation or other means (a relatively common occurrence, usually the result of *psychological* trauma). A subdivision of the second category includes those men who ejaculate only *unconsciously*, as in the following case: "I've never had any trouble getting or maintaining an erection, but have never yet climaxed either in actual intercourse or as a result of masturbation. All my releases are limited to nocturnal emissions, when, of course, I'm asleep—at least until the process has already begun." This man then went on to wonder whether the cause was physical or psychological. Well, if he had made the effort to view his problem objectively, he would have reasoned that (1) he was able to get an erection and maintain it; (2) he had orgasms of *some* kind, therefore (3) his problem clearly was psychological.

Now the male who *occasionally* finds himself unable to reach a climax through lovemaking should try to resolve the condition with a reversal of one of the techniques used for overcoming *premature* ejaculation; just as he might train himself to control ejaculation by conjuring up nonsexual thoughts, so can he draw on erotic fantasies to turn himself on. But if the condition is *chronic*, the man would do well to turn to the treatment developed by Masters and Johnson. The initial stage requires the female partner to *manually* manipulate the male to orgasm, using a moisturizing lotion and asking him which movements feel best. Some women reject this step at first, considering it for male pleasure only—until they realize the more they arouse the man, the more he will concentrate on exciting them, too. (The sexual arena is the prime territory on which to learn that one receives in proportion to what one gives.) And that's why Masters and Johnson emphasize the importance of dealing with the couple as a unit rather than focusing on the male alone.

Next stage in the treatment involves stimulating the man up to just the point of orgasm, then, with the female sitting astride him, having intercourse. Her thrusting pelvic movements will almost surely produce ejaculation if their timing is correct. Once a climax has been reached in this manner, a significant mental block will have been removed—and the subsequent pacing of penetration can continually be altered until normal relations ensue.

As I've noted earlier, *primary* ejaculatory incompetence is a relatively rare condition brought on by physical disorder; therefore, alleviation lies in treating the *cause,* not the problem itself. But so far as curing the more common secondary form of the malfunction, Masters and Johnson have had an 82.4 percent rate of success, a ratio they think will improve as their method becomes more refined.

Impotence: The failure to achieve an erection or to maintain one long enough for intercourse is a common condition which has plagued men— not to mention their women—throughout history. Now I realize you may have heard much of this before, but since fear of impotency *is* such a common male insecurity, let's go through it again: Of the two types of impotence, primary and secondary, the first refers to cases where the man has *never* been able to maintain an erection, and the second to incidences where, after a history of successful experience with intercourse, the man no longer finds it possible to carry through to penetration.

We're talking here about *chronic* impotency, not the *occasional* failure to maintain sexual excitation, which occurs in all men at some time in their lives and is caused, perhaps, by temporary psychic distress, physical fatigue, *over*indulgence in food or alcohol (*immoderate* drinking is one of the best ways to kill off sexual inhibitions), intake of certain drugs, lack of sleep, or a recent prolonged session of lovemaking. (Often, of course, an isolated episode of failure may be so traumatic to a man's ego that he may suffer from that time on the "fear of fear"—so if your man should now and then be less than a tiger, you ought to reassure him you're not particularly upset, nothing is wrong, and that there will be plenty of other opportunities for *amour* . . . just kiss him, snuggle up, and go to sleep.)

But how do you distinguish between an occasional bout of impotency and the chronic secondary type? (About the *primary* form we have no doubt; if a man has *never* maintained an erection, he is impotent—period!) Well, according to Masters and Johnson, "When an individual male's rate of failure at successful coital connection approaches 25 percent of his opportunities, the clinical diagnosis of secondary impotence must be accepted."

When determining causes of this condition, physical factors should be sought first, because they are easiest to diagnose and perhaps to treat. That's why a complete medical examination is imperative in investigating problems of chronic impotency. A doctor will look not only for signs of fatigue, overindulgence, or the other factors mentioned earlier but also hormonal imbalance and disease such as diabetes, of which impotence is often an early symptom. *Then,* if no physical problem can be found and especially if a man has no trouble attaining an erection *except* during intercourse, psychic factors are almost always suspected. A case in point is the twenty-two-year-old college student who put his case to a physician this way: "Whenever I go to bed with a girl, I can't stay aroused long enough to have proper coitus. It's not that I don't get aroused at all, because I do easily. But by the time we're ready for intercourse I lose my erection. When I masturbate, I have no trouble going all the way to orgasm—so I think my potency is all right. But I have girl friends and I'd naturally like to satisfy them. I doubt that my problem's psychological because sex doesn't hang me up. What do you think?" The doctor had to explain that since the only difference for him between success and failure seemed to be the *presence* of a partner, his problem was *clearly* psychological, which should have been apparent to him from his own words.

Many elements can contribute to psychological impotency, including an overbearing mother, rigid religious training, a primarily homosexual orientation, self-deprecation, a developing interest in another woman, or just plain boredom with a sexual partner. And Dr. Donald Hastings, the Minneapolis psychiatrist, in his book *Sexual Expression in Marriage,* has described several forms this condition can take: impotence of inexperience —due to feeling inept, fear of impregnating or hurting the partner, or guilt; impotence only with one's wife, frequently stemming from pent-up feelings of hostility and resentment (on the infrequent occasions when the couple does make love, they've usually been drinking beforehand: there's nothing like a friendly glass to mellow a man for sex, so long as he doesn't imbibe his way to failure); impotence with a loved female, often occurring when the man associates her too closely with his mother.

Once the diagnosis of psychological impotency has been made, treatment should be immediately begun, lest the failure pattern be indefinitely perpetuated. Traditionally, the recommended therapy had been a course of psychoanalysis lasting from months to years and often producing many insights but few erections. Then along came Masters and Johnson with their *clinical* method, a two-week program which stresses treatment of the *couple.* (It's too complicated to go into here, but you can find it fully described in *Human Sexual Inadequacy.*) They've so far had a success rate of 78.8 percent with cases of secondary impotence and 59.4 percent with primary—figures which compare favorably with other methods, but certainly a more productive cure must be discovered. (If only psychological impotency were as easy to erase as physical: a little medication here, a few hormones there, even surgery if indicated—I know the last may sound drastic, but it *works!*)

Some poor-lover symptoms are much less complicated to handle, and usually a few gentle suggestions from you can do the trick:

For the pusher-thruster: Love with him probably doesn't last long, and his fast in-out motions give you minimum sensation. Remark to him that you read the slower the motion, the more friction and tension in the sex organs. You might also play slow music to tone down his tempo.

For the rough petter: Your man loves you, but shows it awkwardly. He handles your breasts like salamis, and just doesn't realize how *tender* your other parts are! Best cure: Have him lie down in darkness. Tell him that you have a surprise for him. Before he lunges, run your fingers— feather-light—from the tips of his toes to his face. Brush him ever so gently. Ask him how it feels. He'll say it's great, and if he's *not* a boob, he'll try the same caresses on you. Exclaim rapturously enough and, hopefully, he'll *never* go back to the grab-bag method.

For the unimaginative lover: Some of the saddest stories I've ever heard were from women who loved (or had learned to love) sex in all its variety, then with touching generosity tried to share their sexuality with a new lover—only to have the *man* recoil in disgust! The awful truth: *Some* men still haven't shed the superstition that sex is *naughty,* that if a "nice" girl *does* it, at least she doesn't do it with enthusiasm, inventiveness, or— heaven forfend!—aggressiveness. As the Victorian sex-maxim went, "Ladies don't *move.*"

If you love him, of course, you'll take the risk, hope he'll be *pleased* that you want to expand your sexual intimacy. Make sure you're both used to each other's bodies . . . touch, look, stroke . . . *before* you suggest any sexual fillips. Suggest gently: "Would you like me to . . . ?" (*Show* him.) Tell him you love him and his nice body, be affectionate and tender. Tell him *he* inspires you to sexy feelings.

Don't tell him how fabulous it was that time Harvey made love to you upside down; *don't* wear black satin stiletto heels or other supersex paraphernalia to bed—you'll only reinforce the "bad girl" myth; *don't* tell him he's hung up and needs twenty thousand dollars worth of psychoanalysis.

Most men *will* respond—perhaps slowly, but keep trying! Only you know where your frustration threshold is; when you reach it, tell him gently *why* you're leaving.

*N*ever use an imperative in bed ("Kiss my breasts!" "Stroke my back!" "Slower, you fool!") *Instead,* say, "I love it when you kiss my breasts" (even if it's never occurred to him). Simply roll over, offer your back for the stroking. (Remember our sensuous pussycat?) When he's hit the pace you like, murmur, "That's perfect . . . that's *exactly* the way I like it."

Do unto a lover as you would have him do unto you. If you like soft, crooning words of love, don't lie there tight-lipped waiting for him to start. Murmur sweet nothings *first* . . . he'll soon reply.

Guide him nonverbally if words would be too blunt; "Stop that! You're killing me!" will destroy the mood. Instead, embrace him suddenly and strongly enough to make him stop whatever dumb thing *he* was doing . . . lead him into something else.

Reward your lover. When he's done something exquisite (*especially* if such finesse is the exception), repay him with tender demonstrations of your love. Don't forget—men have their doubts and fears in bed, too. They don't know *what* you like unless you *respond.* One way to tell him you think he's *fine* is the intricate and varied art of kissing.

It is tougher to be a man now than in the old days when no woman or child dared contradict him. The much larger role women play in the world (not to mention bed) today automatically has whittled down the masculine image a bit. And also because it is usually up to the male to initiate the sexual moves, he feels something like the man who has suggested a new restaurant to a gourmet; all during the meal he's worrying about having made the right choice. But whatever the reason for everyday male insecurity—the state of the world or the pangs from his psyche—a man loves a girl who gives him reassurance about his sexual role . . . who encourages him to be a *man*. And I don't know of a faster way to get a man to act like one than to kiss him.

By kissing him you show you are not inert and passive, quietly and unnervingly sitting in judgment of whatever he's doing. A kiss tells him he's doing the *right* thing . . . that you want him as a man. You actively reassure him, encourage him, arouse him . . . whatever is appropriate to the moment. You can give him a quick, warm, tender, unexpected kiss right there in public if he suddenly feels nervous about meeting new people . . . end a quarrel when words seem to be weaving you both into greater tangles . . . arouse him if he feels tired at the end of the day . . . or lead him to even greater heights later in the evening. Kissing tells him he's a man, and that you're glad of it.

The Hindus or Chinese or some other clever people have apparently thought up 72 (or is it 972?) different ways to make love, but most people usually find only a few of these fun (or even practical). And so, as my friend the romantic said, perhaps a kind of sameness drifts into the act. Not so with kissing. There are many, many ways to vary the manner in which you kiss . . . thus imparting a little novelty you'll both be grateful for. Here are a few ideas:

- Try having a conversation while you kiss; yes, you talk right through the kiss, but mostly in short phrases.
- The inside of the lips is much more sensitive than the part you see when you look at someone. Try to present him with that warm, moist, soft inner lip.
- I once knew a marvelous girl who would seemingly try to swallow my nose whenever she thought I looked depressed. She'd give it a gentle bite . . . I don't know why, but that always made me giggle, and it also felt nice.
- Try putting a finger into his mouth while you kiss, and tickle his tongue with it.
- If you're going to be standing when you kiss, don't move and don't sidestep. Get your kneecaps pointed directly at his, and the rest will be history.
- The corners of his lips are very sensitive—perhaps because they are so rarely touched or used. Put the tip of your tongue (just the tip) into one of these corners. You'll be giving him a tiny, lovely little jolt.
- Confucius say: Sexy girls don't kiss with teeth closed . . . prudes use tongue only to lick postage stamps.
- Next time he kisses you, keep your eyes open. When he opens his and sees you looking lovingly right into them, he'll get a lift . . . you're not kissing a dream or a fantasy man; you're kissing *him*. I predict he'll pull you in even closer for a *second* one.
- A good way to get him to open his eyes is to kiss them.
- Men's nipples grow erect with excitement when you kiss them. Men also like you to kiss the very tips of their fingers.
- Holding his face with your two hands while you kiss is very tender.
- Pushing a grape into his mouth from yours isn't bad at all. If you really love him, chocolate is even better.
- Rubbing noses or kissing noses is very nice. So is kissing the palm of the hand.

- Sometime when he's sitting in a chair, come up behind him and, leaning far forward, give him an upside-down kiss. It's a little hard mechanically, but the sudden surprise may put even better ideas in his head.
- Some men don't like to be bitten hard. There's no rule, but watch it.
- On the beach, on a hot summer day, drink something with ice in it and then immediately kiss his closed eyes.
- When a girl puts her tongue in my mouth, I find it much more stimulating if she does it slowly. The frantic bit is out.
- Ask him to stick his tongue out. Then kiss it.
- A tongue in his ear will often make him shudder with pleasure. But some men don't like that, so be sure he's enjoying it.
- Just plain nibbling on his ear is nice, too.
- Try a butterfly kiss. Put your face as close as you can to his, then flutter your eyelashes. It's sort of a strange, tickly feeling, and you'll both find you're laughing and kissing at the same time.
- Invent some new kisses of your own.

*A*nother way to make your man a better lover (if he already is a pretty good one) is to help him stay in top physical shape. Encourage him to be active in sports and stay trim. The man who feels fit, handsome, and virile makes love better than the man who has to sling a paunch into bed.

Keep your man lean, but well supplied with the foods that will give him energy in bed. Smart women have always known how to keep a man fed, and have learned to use the potent stimulants of certain foods to satisfy one hunger and stimulate another one. Not all the craft of using foods with aphrodisiac properties was developed by chefs hired by jaded old syba-rites, wistfully (and often vainly) trying to light new fires in an empty grate. Through the centuries, from Eve to Cleopatra to Pompadour to Du Barry to *you*, women in love have learned by studying their men which foods will satisfy the stomach and leave a man yawning and torpid, ready only for sleep, and which will satisfy his stomach and leave him with a pleasantly skittish gleam in his eye. As a ghastly example of the former, consider the surfeit of a Thanksgiving dinner, with all its abundance of favorite dishes. Can you imagine anybody feeling like doing *anything* except groaning after such a meal? Conversely, have you noticed how often the male on the hunt (possibly for *you!*) happily gnaws his way through a large rare steak to prepare himself for the evening ahead?

But is anything more aphrodisiac than steak? You bet there is. The classic literature about *la cuisine de l'amour* lists a wild assortment of time-tested favorites that reputedly can be used as erotic stimulants—everything from eels to truffles. Much has been said to extol the oyster; indeed, I know one actor who spent a week in New Orleans dashing into oyster bars with astonishing frequency, to the amusement of his manager. At the time, the manager did not know that the actor had found that a woman already registered as his wife was in his hotel when he arrived. Then his wife descended the next day and was diverted to another hotel. In addition, two other girls had separately flown down from New York "just to be near him." Perhaps the oysters helped; no complaints were heard from any of the ladies—or from the actor, except about his state of exhaustion.

Another sly fellow I know heads instantly for a hangtown fry, consisting of eggs, oysters, and bacon, after a night of exceptional activity. Neither man is a gourmet, yet both are acting instinctively, seeking to restock the body with protein and phosphorus, which the act of love depletes.

Down through recorded history of the lore of love, the same foods keep reappearing: fish, shellfish, caviar, eggs, rare to raw beef, asparagus, mushrooms, truffles, celery, artichokes, honey, chocolate.

*T*oday, we know *why*. Fish and shellfish and eggs are all rich in protein, phosphorus, and trace minerals. Caviar is doubly good because it is both fish *and* eggs! Rare to raw beef is pure protein. And protein is pure *pow!*—the stuff not only to live on but to love on, while phosphorus is considered to be a potent physical stimulus. (No, don't go out and eat a box of matches—their phosphorus is chemically manufactured. We're talking about natural mineral phosphorus found in shellfish and about all the essential trace minerals the body needs for balanced health and continued energy.)

Asparagus, artichokes, mushrooms, and truffles all have strong, earthy fragrances that are subtly suggestive and exciting. Among its other virtues, celery is good for the nerves, calming the jittery, soothing and encouraging the timorous.

Honey and chocolate both convert to instant energy and build up body heat as well. (Skin divers frequently gulp honey and wolf down chocolate.) And then there are all the heady, potent spices (nutmeg, ginger, mace, clove, pepper), which are of themselves stimulants to the taste buds and to the body's functions—but in overuse can also be considered irritants. Add to this list, because of modern refrigeration and transportation, the suave and buttery avocado, unknown to the Old World but definitely *not* to the New. Mexico was probably first to recognize the avocado as an aphrodisiac. Legend reports that all young Aztec girls were confined to the house during the height of the avocado season, lest they go wandering around, shyly murmuring, "Which way to the *ahuacatl?*", which translates loosely as "the testicle tree" and reputedly would be certain later to produce more than one kind of fruit.

By 1672, a traveling Englishman, W. Hughes, wrote of the avocado, " . . . I think it to be one of the most rare and pleasant fruits. . . . It nourisheth and strengtheneth the body, corroborating the vital spirits and procuring lust exceedingly. . . ." Actually, the avocado has eleven vitamins and fourteen basic minerals, no starch or sugar, and an exceptionally high protein (*pow!*) content for a fruit. Contrary to what you may have heard, it *does not have* thousands of calories. The recently revised tables of the U.S. Department of Agriculture list it at 167 calories per 100 grams, which means that half an avocado (the average serving) contains only 150 calories (not bad for the returns it can net!)

*M*any of the classic aphrodisiac foods are basically sensuous, and their appeal is often to more than one of the senses. Obviously, the foods with phallic shapes stimulate through the sense of *sight* by visually stirring the imagination—eels and asparagus, for example. The charm of foods with such ovoid shapes as eggs, artichokes, avocados, and figs, is equally obvious to the eye.

Then there are such *schlurpy*, delicate delights as raw oysters and clams, and the bland, meltingly textured ones like figs and avocados. All of these are wholesome and nourishing in themselves, promoting feelings of well-being, happiness, and relaxation.

Caviar, to me, rings on the palate like music. I would like to bathe in a tub of oysters. And a beautiful blonde singer once told me that the sexiest experience she ever had was on a silly Sunday morning when her husband, in an antic mood, dropped a slice of fresh ripe peach down the front of her negligée and pushed it flat against her skin with his hand. The final result of *that* was a permanently stained robe and a very happy woman.

Thus, food for lovers can take many guises. It can restore and stimulate . . . it can soothe and calm . . . it can be heady or seemingly (but not really) soporific. One wife I know has a high-strung, self-driving artist for a mate. There are days when all he wants for dinner is "pillow food"—something soft and gentle enough not to bruise him should he fall asleep at dinner with his head on his plate. So she makes a delicate chicken fricasee seasoned with celery, bland mashed potatoes enriched with egg, spinach lightly dressed with lemon and a dusting of fresh nutmeg, and, perhaps, a delicate chocolate mousse for dessert. While he gratefully sips an icy, perfect martini before dinner, there is a guacamole of coarsely mashed avocado with the crunch of chopped bacon and an extra dash of Tabasco.

This, then, is "pillow food." Soft, gentle, and relaxing; food to leave a man in a euphoric mood. And it contains seven of the classic aphrodisiac foodstuffs. Somewhat smugly, the lady smiles when I ask her if he *does* go to sleep after such a meal. "Eventually," she murmurs.

So, food for lovers need not be some exotic and expensive concoction containing vast amounts of truffles, eels, or hummingbirds' tongues drenched in honey. Nor does it need a private room in a lush restaurant, lavishly draped in red plush, with a tiny peephole in the door so the waiter can make his service of the meal as discreet as possible. It can be the simplest of everyday fare if prepared with knowledge and care and served with pride and love in what is simply a *peaceful* setting.

And would it surprise you to learn that such sneakily aphrodisiac food is healthy? In the best sense. Webster defines health as "the condition of being sound in mind, body, or soul." So, the food you give a man to bring him to that state is healthy.

The game of love is played by two people. *He* can pursue and woo you with rich, elaborate, expensive meals in so-called sexy settings. This is expected and obvious, since he is the male and *wants* to chase you. What he needn't know is that the artful little dinners *you* feed him are carefully designed to rouse his interest in the chase. That's what aphrodisiacs are all about.

Sick sex

TWELVE

We've been extolling the joys of sex so much you may be feeling "anything goes." Wrong. Not all sex is great, zesty fun. You *can* get trapped in a sexual involvement that can *hurt* you. Sex, which should be glorious, can be twisted into something degrading. It's important to keep your sensuality healthy—aimed at enderness, communication, loving. Alas, the sexual misinformation spread by well-intentioned friends *can* be frightening. People carelessly and *inaccurately* talk about nymphomania, sadism, and masochism . . . but *you* won't be misled if you learn the *facts* about these three sexual aberrations.

Nymphomania: Too Much of a Bad Thing

When a girl flits from one man to another—without much pleasure—she may be a nymphomaniac. Her drive is not real passion, just sick haste; her life, a rumpled search for the right man in the right bed. She'll never *find* him because no man can help her (except a psychiatrist). She's *sick*, not sensual.

The medical literature on nymphomania is sparse, and the experts are not always in agreement. In *Sexual Deviations in the Female*, Dr. Louis London writes: "Nymphomania is not rare, but only a few of the women who have this deviation consult a physican. . . ." Dr. Albert Ellis and Edward Sagarin, in their book, *Nymphomania*, consider that, properly defined, nymphomania applies to only a small number of women. Physiological factors like brain damage, chemical disturbances, and some physical irregularities can cause the condition; but since no *anatomical* anomaly invariably results in compulsive promiscuity, it seems, as Dr. Ellis points out, "that although certain physiological changes may trigger nymphomania, they only do so when *psychological* predispositions in this direction also exist."

There is a difference of opinion as to whether failure to achieve orgasm is the main symptom of nymphomania. If orgasm means release of excitement or sexual climax, then nymphomaniacs can achieve it. But if it means full emotional gratification and contented aftermath, which is what I understand it to mean, then nymphomaniacs do not obtain orgasm, and so are driven to seek more and more sexual experience in their abortive search. To suggest, however, that all women who never achieve orgasm (and there are many) are nymphomaniacal is, of course, absurd. The lack of orgasm can be due to sex always with the wrong person (for her), frigidity or some other neurosis, or (rarely) a physical anomaly. (Incidentally, most of the expert commentators on this very sensitive *female* subject are *men,* which accounts for some of the disputes and for difficulty concerning definition.) It is compulsive promiscuity that really distinguishes the nymphomaniac from the rest. She is a woman impelled by her inner emotional drives to constant repetition of the sexual act, and is always at the mercy of her overwhelming desires. Never free from excitement, she has to have one man after another, sometimes several in one day, who may be complete strangers.

The highly promiscuous woman who is not compulsive reserves for herself both choice and discrimination in opportunity and partners, however numerous her sexual adventures—although her critics may vehemently disagree. The compulsiveness of the nymphomaniac's promiscuity leaves her no choice of action; though she may have some discrimination, she can seldom exercise it. Her excitement is always with her in the same way as thirst is the constant companion of the alcoholic. When her tension mounts unbearably, she has to find a man, just as when the alcoholic's need becomes compelling, he has to get a drink. And just as the alcoholic will drink methylated spirit when all other pipelines are closed, so the nymphomaniac will have intercourse with *any* man when there is no alternative.

At these times, age, physical attraction, mental or class compatibility, race or religion—and personal cleanliness—will have no meaning for her. This knowledge makes her self-disgust even greater than the alcoholic's, because deep down she feels she is doing violence to herself, not only as a person, but as a woman. The more intense her uncontrollable self-propelled sex drive, the more she loathes herself. This is a sexual circle of the most vicious kind, destructive in its progression and abominable in its continuous hangover of poisonous self-denigration.

page 180

Seeds of nymphomania are often sown very early. It can start with an emotionally hungry baby, a child who is never fulfilled because she didn't get from her mother the physical contact all babies crave and urgently need. Cuddling, kissing, handling, which are all expressions of what the "breast" means in a baby's life, were dangerously missing from hers. The causes are infinite. She may have been separated from her mother by absence or death; her mother may have been a compulsive careerist with no time for the baby, or a socialite whose other activities took priority. Her mother may not have wanted her, disliked her at birth, or found physical demonstration of affection repellent. This is not a matter of blame-pointing—since circumstances or individuals usually force these situations—but of fact. And whether the deprivation was voluntary or involuntary, conscious or unconscious, the effect on the baby is the same.

By the age of three or four, intense excitement is usually harbored in these children. Often, they masturbate earlier (sometimes at six months) and much more than other children. This is a measure of the degree of unrequited stimulation that is only resolved by self-comforting for want of something better. The unappeased longing, for such a child, increases, and a deep sense of anger and hostility builds up against her mother as the baby grows into a fiercely hungry and bitterly resentful little girl. This hunger is transferred to her father when he begins to exist for her (much later than her mother), and in late childhood or puberty she almost literally throws herself at him.

If her father discourages her exaggerated demands for physical contact, which he almost inevitably does, she sees this as a complete rejection of herself, and her anger swerves from her mother to her father. If her father unconsciously responds with encouragement and a flirtatious relationship is established, her stimulation is greatly enhanced, but gratification is still blocked and she feels rejected. In either case, she has suffered a double injury, first from mother and then from father, and the nymphomaniac pattern for this child is set.

Her raging need is now a greedy monster to be appeased only by sexual intercourse. Although probably only in her early teens, she will seek this outlet feverishly and resort to sex play with other girls or masturbation when it is not available. Sex serves a double purpose for the nymphomaniac: a constant search for fulfillment, and the unending means of punishing men, for whom her father is the prototype. Unconsciously, she is looking for the ideal man who will give her gratification. But since man is no longer a person to her, but a vehicle for revenge and the rehabilitation of her troubled ego, she never finds him. So her compulsive search is continuous and loveless, full of intense sexual activity but without any permanent satisfactions.

In many case histories of nymphomaniacs, stress is put on various factors: A girl may have had a too-repressive upbringing, a too permissive one, or she may have been sexually abused. She may be crying out for love or desperately seeking acceptance and approval, or too much may be expected of her. All these figments of insecurity add to the original injury or have grown out of it, but they are not the primary cause. Even the important relationship with her father is secondary to the early nonfulfillment.

Like all personalities, nymphomaniacs exhibit individual characteristics in the way they behave. Some are aggressive in their conquests and subsequent method of disposal (like the Don Juan), while others rapidly move on, frightened that unless they do, the man will leave them first. Some nymphomaniacs are exhibitionists, while others are demure in dress and behavior. But whatever the particular character structure, the nymphomaniac's basic motivations are always the same: lack of early affection, and the need to punish men.

Since a woman's self-esteem is bound up with her sexual role, if she feels incomplete sexually, she feels worthless as a person. Many women share these feelings of sexual inadequacy but manage to sublimate them by diving into acute domesticity, concentrating on their children, or following a career. Others have a creative hobby, intense social activities, or community and club work that helps fill the gap. The nymphomaniac has none of these alternatives since her method of compensation is, paradoxically, to go on trying to get satisfaction out of the very occupation that always lets her down and leaves her feeling like a creature of no value. She is the supreme example of bashing one's head against a brick wall— although it's not her head that gets ruthlessly damaged, but her ego. How the pattern develops is described in the following two cases:

Janet was born in England during World War II. Her father worked in London, and her mother sent her to a residential nursery in the country. She stayed there four years, then went to her grandmother until her parents found an apartment and her brother was born. Janet was now six, a difficult child. She alternated between smothering her small brother with affection, and spite—because she felt her parents made too much fuss over him.

As she got older, she attached herself to her father, always sitting on his lap, trying to get into the bathroom with him, and slipping into his bed.

Finding her behavior embarrassing and strange, her father pushed her from him, constantly telling her to behave. Janet felt he didn't want her and did everything she could to annoy him. She began running around with a gang of boys and girls older than herself, and soon found that if she let the boys do what they liked to her, she was accepted. By thirteen she was having sexual intercourse with anyone who wanted her to, and when her horrified parents found out, they packed her off to boarding school. But before long she was expelled for her extracurricular sexual activities.

Home again, she became more circumspect in her behavior and her parents persuaded themselves she had settled down. She was married at seventeen and they were delighted and relieved. But after a few months she started sleeping with other men and didn't seem to care when her husband found out. He was very fond of her, and their marriage continued for a few years, punctured by constant rows, until finally he left her. Janet went to another town. Her parents have not heard from her since.

Another example: Katherine's mother had a business that needed her close attention, so a succession of au pair girls or mother's helpers looked after Katherine from birth. When her mother returned at night, Katherine was asleep and the girls complained she was "dirty, always playing with herself." Sundays her mother had too much to do at home to spare much time for her, and anyhow she was not a demonstrative woman. When Katherine transferred her attention to her father, he was entranced and flattered by this young daughter who clung to him, and he made a great fuss over her.

By her early teens, she was following the same pattern as Janet, and her parents were seriously worried. Advised by their doctor they took her to a psychiatrist. After several sessions he explained to them what was happening and that the only way they could help Katherine was to give her complete sexual freedom while showing her all the love they could, and at the same time letting her continue psychiatric treatment. They were shocked at the "cure," but agreed, as they felt they had no choice if Katherine was to get well. The next few years were extremely difficult for them all, but gradually her wild promiscuity ceased. Now Katherine is married, has two children and is on good terms with her parents.

The emotional crippling of children is one of the sicker features of our society, and nymphomania is one of the ways this sickness manifests itself. But since children (and parents) are not all alike, every girl who has suffered this early deprivation of affection does not invariably become a nymphomaniac. Sometimes the neurosis takes another form; sometimes a mother-substitute (usually a relative or nurse) provides the physical loving; sometimes the original injury is righted during puberty and so not compounded. Sometimes children emerge miraculously unscathed, protected by one of the imponderables that make up the unique quality of human beings. Once an adult, however, the nymphomaniac does not usually seek help until the other facets of her havoc-ridden life are nullified by her compulsion—and not always then.

Just as our society creates emotional cripples, so our social attitudes, which are often extremely contradictory, add to the misery and sickness. One has only to look at the guilt and shame associated with masturbation, which is a normal part of a child's healthy development and the sole sexual outlet, however inadequate, for many adults—to see one example of our malaise. It takes love, understanding, and courage for parents to see (as Katherine's did) that their daughter would never be a healthy woman unless she were permitted to find the gratification she desperately needed, even if it meant outraging the conventions they had always accepted. Fear of social stigma makes parents give priority to covering up the problem rather than recognizing it and getting help to deal with it. And the same fear causes adult nymphomaniacs to behave the same way.

The feeling that there is something degrading about women who seek sex overtly is responsible for nymphomaniacs being wrongly equated with prostitutes, rather than with the deeply disturbed—which they are. In fact, few prostitutes are nymphomaniacs, and nymphomaniacs seldom make successful prostitutes. The latter consider the former contemptibly unprofessional, since their compulsiveness destroys the essential financial side of these transactions. To many men, however, the difference is distinctly blurred. When they transfer the fantasy of making love to an exciting, sexually voracious woman to the reality of a prostitute, they hope the prostitute will be nymphomaniacal. If they're sincere, they are often disappointed! This fantasied need expresses a man's fear of his own sexual inadequacy, and men who go to the lengths of marrying a nymphomaniac unconsciously see in her intense demands the sexual push they lack themselves. Even the "sharing" necessitated by his wife's extramarital activities can be reassuring when it relieves him of some of his deeply feared sexual responsibilities without great loss of prestige. After all, anyone married to a nymphomaniac has a good alibi if he cannot respond to her sexual demands.

Yet a man can rarely stand either the punishing promiscuous pace or living with a woman who is so disturbed that she is incapable of love or forming a human relationship. His love and support, even if they survive, are seldom sufficient to help her find a way out of her sexual morass. Psychiatric help, however, backed by his stamina, courage and patience may do the trick—but not always. There is a considerable recovery rate in many cases of nymphomania and partial success in more; it is tragic if a woman feels her situation to be so hopeless and shameful (as many do) that rather than take her illness to a doctor, she limps through life a sick woman—bereft of all self-esteem.

But cure is not instant. Indeed, through analytical treatment, a patient may come to understand what happened to her and why, but that is only the start. She often finds it hard to let go of her deep anger and resentment toward those who injured her. As Dr. Ellis points out, people do not always want to change their early parental conditioning, and cling leechlike to their hostility. They cannot relinquish placing the blame and keeping it there—although the damage was probably unconsciously done. Yet until they lose the *need* to blame, they won't lose their nymphomania. However, this is not a point of complete despair, since more aggressive therapy (Dr. Ellis uses a method he calls *rational-emotive*) has succeeded in some cases where psychoanalysis had failed.

Sado-Masochism: Misery Loves Company

Sadism and masochism are two variations on the same theme: *pain*. The sadist delights in inflicting sexual cruelty . . . the masochist thrives on receiving it! People who are involved in sado-masochistic sex often say, "There is a thin line between pain and pleasure." We don't think it's as *thin* as all that. Whips, chains, red welts, black-and-blue marks, degrading insults—these emblems of pain don't belong in the bedroom.

Not all sadists and masochists inflict or welcome *bodily* pain. Some men and women torment each other *emotionally*, twisting the normal sexual pattern of love and tenderness to their own needs. These warped lovers prefer humiliation to pleasure, degradation to elevating joy. The girl who sleeps with a man who repeatedly hurts her (by philandering or insulting her) is at the whip's end just as surely as if she were living the *Story of O.* And the woman who calls her lover less than a man, who makes him feel impotent—she's as castrating as a sadist with a knife in her hand.

Sado-masochism forms a shadowy subculture. Certain symbols—leather, suede, boots, studs—brand the more blatant practitioners. (*No,* your studded garrison belt from Paris will *not* beckon slavish lovers longing to be beaten to a pulp . . . unless you head for an S&M gathering place.) More subtle sado-masochists (who may not even realize they *are* sado-masochists) find each other through trial and error. But meet they do: The sadist *requires* the masochist, and vice versa (although in dire need a clever sado-masochist can manipulate *circumstances* to cause pain to himself or others). The sado-masochistic relationship exaggerates the tradition of male-female, dominant-submissive sex roles (which many people now believe are abnormal under *any* circumstances!)

If you feel you've been drawn into sado-masochistic patterns, run, don't walk, to the nearest shrink. You don't want to wait until you've outgrown this troubled behavior (like when you're seventy years old), do you?

There are many other forms of sexual "perversion" (an unfortunately derogatory word that implies a self-righteous moral judgment)—but we don't expect you'll run up against many of them in your personal sex life. Voyeurs and exhibitionists aren't looking for involvement; fetishists and transvestites tend to keep their own company or that of others who share their preferences. None of these people are likely to hurt you even if you *do* encounter them.

The "sick sex" that *can* hurt you is the creeping variety of unsatisfactory entanglement that's become a *crutch*. It's so easy to be seduced into a sick pattern and *stay* there once you get *dependent* on it. The man may appear charming, virile, intelligent . . . and by the time you find out he *despises* women or is *using* you for some twisted purpose, it might just be too late. If you find yourself crying and tearing your hair over a man—*no more!* Love should be a celebration. Find someone you can tickle, giggle with, and enjoy in bed. You'll have more fun!

*Continuing
to live
sensuously*

THIRTEEN

By now, you have become truly in touch with your body—and *his*. Every physical act, even the tiniest and most ordinary, is now a vital pleasure. An aura of *life* surrounds you, and great things are beginning to happen. First: You enjoy living more. Second: People enjoy *you* more. You're relaxed, open to new experience . . . your sensuality softens and enhances all you do.

Where do you go from here? How to keep *growing?* Here is the philosophy of one woman's life-style:

> "I choose a new color each birthday, and I have been known to celebrate more than one birthday a year mostly when I move and want to color my life all new. In my pink period, which followed on the heels of my black period, I used to emphatically say, "I must live in pink, it does great things for my looks and outlook." That year I got smooth silk sheets in an aristocratic powder pink, and what's more they were embroidered with pink English roses. I practically lived in a passionately pink thing that was floor-length and rustled like a Japanese mobile in the wind. My dishwasher got the Chinese pink treatment, too.
>
> "It's amazing but true; that year I looked marvelous in pink, sort of in bloom all the time. Then, when powder pink suddenly looked dusty and washed out, I knew it was time to change. Now I live in stop-white with emerald green touches. It gives me a *serene* sense, a pure-white, above-it-all feeling. See, that's how it is with colors. Could you ever express your

sensuous moods in a more charming and understated way? I like "beige tea" instead of tea with milk. I don't have my coffee black, I drink it dangerously dark. I'd rather be taken to a romantically red place instead of the usual where-every-body-goes place for an after-theater supper. I prefer silver, glisteny caviar with a sharp-yellow slice of lemon, and pale canary-colored champagne from a clear-crystal goblet over any dull, normal assortment of no-color foods. I just like the idea of eating what looks visually exciting so I can thrill two senses at the same time. Moreover, I have seasonal ap-petites. There's absolutely nothing like tiny wild strawberries with their heavenly perfume served on succulent green leaves in the midst of winter first thing when you open your eyes on a clear Sunday morning. *Quelle sensation!* You don't know what to taste first, expecially if he who serves them looks as luscious as the strawberries.

"Oh colors! They are simply made for working girls. Just thinking of my new favorites, I can see a white-white floor-length marabou coat in which to make an entrance. Should it be for the opening of the opera? I see serenely white invitations—engraved, of course—to come to all sorts of illustrious happenings. I see winter vacations in the pure-white surroundings of some mad, marv European skiing resort. I see myself with slightly longer hair, my new eyes in a more romantic mood in tune with my transparently white skin. I see me in white milk baths while talking through a white telephone, and I can practically smell the new pure lily-white perfume in which I shall move. In short, I am ready for the wondrous white world.

"Believing in white—that's thinking sensuously. It takes very special moments and places to think sensuously. To me it happens mostly in the tub, mostly after midnight, and some-times lying in bed, wrapped in the cuddliest of all cashmere sweaters that's too big but I love it madly because it was given to me by someone who adored me utterly or still does. A giant sweater belongs in every working girl's survival kit. The only point is, how to make him part with his favorite cashmere. My last pearl-gray vicuna—which is shamefully soft and by sheer existence makes my cashmeres feel very middle-class—was wrapped around me recently in the French countryside. It happened after dinner. The ceilings were cathedral-high, the demitasse cups were sèvres. The windows to the lush gardens were wide open so that the crisp, fresh country air could rush in freely. I felt slightly chilly in my sleeveless white dress with emerald stripes. Vicuna simply had to come. It was the obvious, the natural answer, the soft touch which I am all for, especially in the case of working girls.

"That's why working girls should concentrate on collecting things soothingly soft—cashmeres instead of stiff nighties; silky, sable-lined raincoats to forget the dreariness of the weather; soft sofas that give; soft scents to live in; soft, pastel-colored chamois wraps around their ever-growing stock portfolios—soft treats of all kinds. Who wants to sleep on foam-padded pillows if you can dream on eiderdown? The idea of living the soft life is terribly becoming to a girl and rather sensuous. The thing is, it's even more becoming when carried through all phases of a working girl's life. Now, it'd be a terrible faux pas if you suddenly put on a record as brash as "Seventy-six Trombones" while he just looked at you meaningfully over his Château Lafitte '61. My audio tastes run mostly toward Baroque music. I find Boccherini enchanting and Purcell elevating.

"Me, I believe intensely in what I do and say. I have opinions and I state them. Things happen in, around and to me. Always. I'm happening from minute to minute. I live through my senses; I don't just use them occasionally. I react spontaneously, innately. I know I cannot control a man's feelings and I don't try to do so. At best, I can understand them, and even that, rarely. But I do understand my own feelings and live quite happily with them. I say what I feel and I make sure I am heard. I tell a man frankly that I intend to be made happy, not miserable, and that I have no yearning for suffering. It's my working-girl thesis and it seems to work for me."

You will find your own style of sensuous growth. One way you'll grow will be *chronologically* . . . but you will age well, be one of the *soft*, certain women, not the hard, anxious ones. In many ways, you won't reach your peak until late maturity, for sensuality improves with time . . . mellows. Each pleasure will deepen the curve of your smile, add calm to your gaze, grace to your body. You will be loved—loved well. And the act of love will nourish you, pamper you.

How much love will you enjoy in a lifetime? How many lovers? It doesn't matter if you know one man or a hundred: The quality of your loving will enrich your experience. You may ripen with the knowledge that you have thrilled and been thrilled by stripling youths, dignified statesmen, powerful magnates, husky athletes . . . or savor the love-time spent with a husband of thirty years, whose desire you've known how to keep, who still awakes your own fires.

If you become a mother, you will be loving, for you understand the importance of a gentle caress, tender hug, unexpected kiss. You won't stifle your exploring, clingy-fingered babies. They will hug your breast and reach out eagerly for the rest of the world.

Certainly, you will have many friends. They will warm themselves by you—for you know how to greet them with a kiss, an embrace, a whispered greeting. Everything about you will radiate physical appeal.

*H*ow to do it? Keep up the practices you've learned in this book. Enhance your love lessons from your own experience. Never neglect your body, but don't fear the soft wrinkles that may come with age. Laugh lines, crow's feet—all can be beautiful markings on a mature woman. Only a frown will distort your face, and you will rarely frown.

Do make a real effort to keep your body supple. Sex will help: Desire makes the hormones flow, keeps you younger, longer.

Watch the young—not with a hawk-eyed envy or desperation to *copy,* but with openness to their fresh enchantments, their new ideas. Keep your looks flexible as they do: You may become a blonde next year, or wear shoulder-length tresses in 1980. Don't ossify into the way you look *now.* Eat health foods. Exercise. *Read* those interviews with mature international beauties who tell about *their* regimens . . . adapt what you wish.

Mainly, stay *open* to experiences. See as much of the world as you can . . . and savor it. Meet new people, give them *all* a chance. Continue to read, to try the new. In short, live life full and hard.

*Y*ou will grow into the kind of woman who makes *younger* girls look shallow and uninteresting, for you will epitomize *woman. Eve. Jeanne Moreau. Marlene Dietrich.* When other women, with less confidence, suffer jealousy and neurosis, you will still glow on, serene with inner light and mystery. Teach others your arts of love, and in so doing, learn them again.

Men will nestle into your tenderness, return to you . . . again and again. To love. For you will give so much love and receive so much love, that in the end you will be made of it. Soft, gossamer: love.

Index

The text of this book
is set in 10 point Palatino
with 2 points leading,
using swash initials
at random.
Chapter numbers
are Bartuska Ebon Open,
and chapter titles
are 14 point Palatino italics
with swash initials, set solid.
Palatino is the creation
of type designer Herman Zapf,
a brilliant German calligrapher.
Bartuska Ebon (both open and regular),
designed by Frank Bartuska
for Photo-Lettering, Inc.,
are used on the jacket,
cover, and title pages.

Jacket design
Don Davenport

Photograph
J. Frederick Smith

Book design
Dorris Crandall

Line drawings
Edward Klauck

Composition
Book Graphics, Inc.